STRATHCLYDE UNIVERSITY LIBRARY

30125 00000824 2

D1493214

THE ROYAL TECHNICAL COLLEGE

LIBRARY

GLASGOW

ROOF BOSSES

ANDERSONIAN LIBRARY
★
WITHDRAWN
FROM
LIBRARY STOCK
★
UNIVERSITY OF STRATHCLYDE

Exeter, nave; The Murder of St Thomas of Canterbury

ROOF BOSSES
IN
MEDIEVAL CHURCHES

AN ASPECT OF GOTHIC SCULPTURE

BY

C. J. P. CAVE
M.A., F.S.A.

ILLUSTRATED
WITH
TELEPHOTOGRAPHS

CAMBRIDGE
AT THE UNIVERSITY PRESS
1948

17032
9-1-50

Printed in Great Britain at the University Press, Cambridge
(Brooke Crutchley, University Printer)
and published by the Cambridge University Press
(Cambridge, and Bentley House, London)

Agents for U.S.A., Canada, and India: Macmillan

Δ
726.59
CAV

729.34

CONTENTS

ILLI
QUAE NISI ADIUVISSET
HOC OPUS NEQUE INCEPTUM
NEQUE CONFECTUM ESSET

PREFACE

THIS STUDY of roof bosses began rather by chance. The carvings in the roof of the quire of Winchester Cathedral had always attracted me from the first time I saw them, and many years later it occurred to me that they would be convenient objects on which to make experiments in telephotography. Having been to some extent successful in this I turned my attention to roof bosses in other places, to find that hidden away, often in semi-darkness, there was a vast array of medieval sculpture in cathedral and church, almost unknown even to those who knew the churches best.

The result of my photographic survey is a collection of over eight thousand telephotographs, the great majority being of roof bosses. In this book I have tried to give a representative selection, with examples not only from cathedrals and great churches but from small parish churches as well. Thus inevitably a large number of important bosses have had to remain unillustrated. I have perhaps given a rather large number of examples of foliate heads, but I wanted to lay stress on these figures, for I feel that the motif had some definite meaning and was not just a fancy of the carver. Also I may have given too many examples of foliage bosses, but I wanted to illustrate the evolution of foliage sculpture, as seen on roof bosses, through the whole of the Gothic period.

I am acutely aware of how much still remains to be recorded and even discovered. I have a list of over a hundred churches where I know or suspect that there are roof bosses worth photographing. I have examined the cathedrals, but I know nothing of parish churches over a great part of the country, and even those counties that I know best have only been partially explored. Friends have told me of many churches where I should find roof bosses, others I have found by my own explorations, but there must be hundreds more of which I know nothing. It is my hope that this book may awaken an interest in the subject and result in the recording of many more roof bosses.

I am greatly indebted to the deans of our cathedrals for so willingly giving me permission to photograph, and in particular to the Dean of Winchester, and to Dr Cranage, late Dean of Norwich. I should like too especially to mention the late Canon T. G. Gardiner of Canterbury for his hospitality on so many occasions in his house in the Precincts, where now, alas, there is only a bomb crater, and for enabling me to photograph in the cathedral at any hour of the day or night that might suit me, for a spot light enables daylight to be dispensed with. I am also much indebted to the late Prebendary H. E. Bishop of Exeter, and to Mr L. E. Tanner, keeper of the archives at Westminster Abbey, for help and advice on many occasions.

I must also put on record the great help given to me by the late Dr M. R. James whom I used to visit periodically at Eton with conundrums that he was almost sure to solve.

And I must express my gratitude to the vergers and caretakers of so many cathedrals and churches for the very real practical assistance they have given me so often and so ungrudgingly, and in this connection I should like to mention especially Winchester, Exeter and Tewkesbury.

C. J. P. C.

March 1948

CHAPTER I

GENERAL SURVEY

THE IMPORTANCE of roof bosses has only been appreciated quite recently. Owing to their position they have not only remained undisturbed during periods of iconoclasm, but they have partially escaped the ravages of the nineteenth-century restorer. Thus, in many cathedrals and churches, almost all the medieval sculpture has perished save the roof bosses and the high corbels. The Lady Chapel at Ely is a classic example; out of the thousands of figures that ornamented the arcading around the walls only one head remains; in the roof bosses not one head has been destroyed.

The reason for their preservation has also been the reason for their neglect. They are usually so high up that the naked eye reveals nothing; field-glasses show up some detail, though a prolonged study of a roof with field-glasses is very tiring to eye and neck. But there are many roofs where field-glasses are of no avail owing to the small amount of light that falls upon them. The great series of bosses in the nave at Tewkesbury is practically invisible except on extremely bright days, and the choir of angels under the soffits of the six lancet-windows in the north transept of Westminster Abbey is quite invisible from the floor even on the very brightest of days.

But roof bosses have not been completely ignored. Dean Goulburn in 1876 published a sumptuous volume dealing with the roof bosses in the nave of Norwich Cathedral, with photographs of each bay, and enlarged photographs of the more important bosses. The photographs are naturally not as good as those that can be taken to-day, but when it is remembered that they must have been taken on wet plates the work is really a *tour de force*. The bosses of Exeter Cathedral were described by Miss Prideaux in 1910; the illustrations are no better, if as good as those from Norwich, but it must be remembered that the latter were taken from scaffolding, the former from the floor. With the exception of a previous brochure on the bosses of Exeter by W. Cotton, F.S.A. (1900), these are the only two books that have appeared on the subject, but there has been a number of papers in the journals of archaeological societies, mostly dealing with bosses in cloisters or in chapels with low roofs where they

could be studied with comparative ease. The late Dr M. R. James wrote papers
on the bosses in the cloisters at Norwich and on those in the Bauchon Chapel in
the same cathedral; R. Griffin described the heraldic bosses in the cloisters at
Canterbury, and W. H. St John Hope those in the Divinity Schools at Oxford.
If we add Canon Wilson's account of the bosses in the cloisters at Worcester,
and that of the Rev. E. Venables on those in the cloisters at Lincoln, we
practically exhaust what has been written until quite recently.

The neglect of the subject was ended by the progress that has been made in
photography; plates and films have improved in speed and in quality; lenses and
especially telephoto lenses have also advanced enormously. But perhaps what
is even more important is that it is now possible, with a portable electric lamp,
to throw a beam of light directly on to the object to be photographed. It is
quite easy now to take a photograph of a roof boss, or other high-up sculpture
or painting even after dark with an exposure of only about 30 sec., and with
such clearness that cobwebs 60 or 70 ft. up come out quite distinctly in the
photographs.

This facility with which photographs can be taken of objects that are only to
be seen with difficulty, if at all, has quite revolutionized the study of roof bosses
and other objects. The telephoto lens and the portable electric spotlight will
have to take their place more and more in the armoury of the archaeologist.

A roof boss is the keystone of the vaulting-ribs. It is important to realize how
it was put in place. The ribs were built up with the aid of centering to the point
where they were ready for the keystone; this was then gradually lowered down
from above, probably with the aid of wedges. In some early examples the
mouldings of the ribs were carried across the boss, and this carving was
probably done after the boss was in place, for had it been carved previously it
would have been extremely difficult to ensure an exact fit, and as a general rule
the fit is absolutely exact, so that part at any rate of the carving, and possibly all
of it, must have been done after the boss had been put in its place. This too has
been done in modern times. I have been told in almost the same words by the
late Mr Adams, who worked for many years in Norwich Cathedral, and by
the late Mr E. Luscombe, clerk of the works at Exeter Cathedral, and himself
a practical mason and carver, that in their opinion the bosses in their cathedrals
were carved *in situ*, and they both had opportunities of seeing the bosses at
close quarters. Mr Luscombe had to superintend the building of a few bays of
the cloisters at Exeter, and himself carved the bosses after they were in place;

but he was also instructed to insert a few old bosses which had survived; he told me that he had far more difficulty with these bosses than with all the new ones put together.

The only important building where there is not a proper fit between vaulting-rib and boss is Lincoln Cathedral; here, in St Hugh's quire and in the nave and transepts, the fit is very clumsy, and indeed in many cases there is no attempt to make a proper fit, and it is quite possible that these bosses were carved in the workshop. It is curious that there is one boss, in the south-west transept, whose carving is only partly finished (329).[1]

In Durham Cathedral one boss, at the east end of the quire, shows signs that a miscalculation was made, for its edge projects downwards well below the level of the vaulting-ribs, and no attempt has been made to carry the rib-mouldings onto the boss as has been done on the other bosses of the quire. Once lowered into its place it would have hardly been practicable to take it out again, and the mistake was such that it was not worth rectifying since from the floor it is quite inappreciable and is only revealed by photography.

A keystone is often of considerable size and without ornamental carving it would look rather heavy; there is no doubt that carved roof bosses do improve the look of a vaulted roof even though the details are not visible to those in the church below. But the medieval craftsman carved his design with as great a care as though it were intended to be seen at close quarters. This, of course, is not really surprising; it is a general characteristic of medieval art, and there are numberless details in cathedrals and churches, in triforium arcades and in clerestories, and indeed on the capitals of the main arcades, which, without optical aid, are quite unapparent from the floor below. But though one might expect to find foliage well carved on a boss where its detail cannot be seen it is certainly surprising to find all sorts of figures, scenes from the Old and the New Testaments, figures of saints, kings, queens, bishops, craftsmen so placed that they could never be seen by the naked eye, except on the rare occasions when cleaning or repairs were in progress, and then only by those engaged on the work.

Some of the detail that is found on bosses is very minute; in the transepts at Norwich there are several compositions in which figures are represented with books in their hands, and on the pages of the books lines and dots represent writing; the subjects of these bosses cannot possibly be made out from the floor

[1] The references are to the illustrations following page 83.

without the aid of glasses; hence the books themselves are invisible and one
wonders at such details as writing being included at all.

In thirteenth-century buildings, such as the early parts of Westminster Abbey
and the Angel quire at Lincoln, the bosses on the high vault are carved with
foliage, while those in the aisles have a certain number of figures, as though the
carvers realized that the high bosses were too far off for detail to be seen while
those in the aisles would be more visible; yet even such low-down bosses cannot
really be seen with ease, and in some cases it is so dark that the details cannot be
seen at all; the numberless people who walk through the aisles of Westminster
Abbey are quite unaware of the curious heads, the centaur, the grotesque bird,
and other figure subjects under which they pass (226-9).

The custom of carving the keystone of a vault originated in Norman times,
though it did not become common till later. In many cases of Norman vaulting
the carving of the ribs is continued across the keystone with no other ornament.
Occasionally, however, small carvings occur on the plain surface at the point of
intersection; a beast's head is so found in the north aisle at Peterborough (178),
and some conventional foliage in the north aisle of the quire at Christ Church,
Oxford. Sometimes there is a small roundel in the middle with carving within,
as in the remarkable sexpartite vaulting at Tickencote (1), where the roundel
encloses three heads, one human and two of beasts. Sometimes an exceedingly
small circle of conventional leaves is found at the centre of the keystone as at
Hemel Hempstead, where such an ornament surrounds a small hole in the
centre.

But even before the advent of Gothic architecture the carving on roof bosses
had become more important than a mere small ornament in the centre of the
keystone, and many examples occur in which the whole lower surface of
the keystone is carved. Perhaps the most remarkable of all the Norman bosses
is the one in the Treasury of Canterbury Cathedral (5); round the outer edge is
a ring of alternate triangles and semicircles, each ornamented with a conventional leaf pattern; within, and forming the base of the triangles and semicircles, is a cable-moulding, and within this are four heads, chin to chin. The
heads are badly drawn and are extremely grotesque, whether purposely or not
it is impossible to say. This boss is important as it is the only one remaining
from Conrad's quire, if indeed there were any others. The design of the four
heads may be older than this, but as a motif it went on right through the Gothic
period. In the Treasury undercroft there are some very curious bosses which

look as though some completely unskilled workman had tried his hand on them, taking his design from the boss in the building above. Four noses with eyes on each side surround a common circular mouth with teeth round it in a circle.[1]

Several small Norman churches have carvings on the keystones which are more elaborate than the small ornaments mentioned above. Tickencote is one example (1); others are to be found at Elkstone (3), where a strap-pattern in the centre is surrounded by four human heads, foreheads inwards; at Iffley (2) a coiled dragon in the centre is surrounded by small heads looking inwards; at Kilpeck (4) there are four grotesque heads, either animal or human, it is not clear which.

There are two large Norman bosses in the chapter-house of Bristol Cathedral (7, 8); one of them has three whorls of a regular leaf-like pattern, the other has a whorl of leaves surrounded by a cable-moulding. In the entrance to the chapter-house there are several small bosses of approximately the same date; on one we find whorls of a leaf-like pattern, on another cable-moulding, and on a third an interlacing strap-pattern.

The above includes all the carved bosses of Norman date that I have hitherto come across.

It was not till Gothic architecture was developed that roof bosses became a matter of course. The keystones at first were usually carved with small conventional leaves, the actual carvings being smaller in diameter than the width of the vaulting-ribs. Examples of such carvings may be seen at Abbey Dore and in the aisles of the quire at Pershore (6).

But the real beginning of large roof bosses in the new style was in the quire at Canterbury, and here we are fortunately able to date them exactly owing to the account of the rebuilding of the quire that has come down to us from the pen of Gervase. But whence the craftsmen of William of Sens got their ideas is not apparent. The carvings at Sens itself are quite small and unimportant; they are hardly more important than those at Abbey Dore and in the aisles at Pershore, and it can hardly have been from Sens that the rich conventional foliage of Canterbury originated. Nevertheless, there are twelfth-century churches in France where roof bosses have elaborate carvings of conventional foliage, sometimes with figures of angels; there are a few examples at Vézelay and Laon,[2] but I am under the impression that such bosses are very rare and that most of the

---

[1] Someone, possibly a boy, has scratched other separate mouths under each nose.
[2] See Viollet-le-Duc, *Dictionnaire Raisonné de l'Architecture Française*, vol. III, pp. 257 ff.

early French bosses are flat plaques. If William of Sens got his ideas from some
church in France, he was no slavish copyist but developed his own style of roof
boss at Canterbury, which William the Englishman later took over and trans-
formed. But wherever the ideas originated, Canterbury seems to have set the
fashion to the rest of England, and almost all subsequent buildings in this
country had their keystones carved with foliage or figures in a style quite
distinct from that which was developed on the Continent.

The early bosses at Canterbury are mainly carved with stiff but very rich
conventional foliage (320, 321); in some cases the leaves radiate straight out from
the centre, in others they run spirally outwards. There are only four bosses in
the quire that have any sculpture other than foliage and fruit; at the west end
of the aisles are two bosses which have dragon-like beasts among the foliage,
and there is one boss with a 'toothache' face, but this is probably a later
addition. In the centre of the eastern crossing is one of the outstanding bosses
in the country (60)—the Agnus Dei, the lamb with a cross-bearing nimbus, and
with the cross and banner of the Resurrection; the boss is surrounded by four
angels, one in each of the angles formed by the vaulting-ribs; this boss is
typically French in feeling; the Agnus Dei is rarer in the south of England than
it is across the Channel; angle figures are very common in France but comparatively rare in England, and angels occur on a number of early French roof
bosses. From the west end of the quire William of Sens had been responsible
for the rebuilding, but in 1178 he had the accident which deprived the
monastery of his services, and the work further east was completed under
William the Englishman. On the high vault we find an immediate change of
style in the roof bosses; we still have conventional foliage but it is no longer the
stiff foliage of the first period of the rebuilding, but a much freer trefoil foliage
which seems to be the precursor of that which dominated English foliage
sculpture for the next hundred years (322, 323).

The bosses in the eastern crypt date from 1180 and though they must have
been put up under William the Englishman they lack the grace of the bosses at
the east end of the high vault, and rather resemble those in the quire aisles. It is
of course quite possible that many of the craftsmen who had worked under
William de Sens remained on under his successor, and that it was only in the
high vault that a new hand was employed.

I have dealt thus in detail with Canterbury because of its great importance in
the history of roof sculptures. That it set the fashion for England I have little

doubt. And this is hardly to be wondered at seeing that Becket's shrine became a place of national pilgrimage, and that many of those who built other cathedrals and churches must have seen and admired the work that had been lavished on the vaulting at Canterbury.

Nevertheless, the actual style of the Canterbury bosses cannot be traced in many other buildings. It is only the general idea of richly carved roof bosses that seems to have spread. There are, however, a few churches where the style of Canterbury may perhaps be discerned. In the chancel at Crondall in Hampshire there is an Agnus Dei (70) and a foliage boss which may even have been carved by some craftsman of William de Sens. In the early bosses at Chichester (332), at Havant, in the church of St Thomas of Canterbury (now the Cathedral) and in the chancel of the church of Saints John and Nicholas (now the Garrison Chapel) at Portsmouth, and in the chancel of St Mary, Guildford, are bosses which seem to me to bear some considerable resemblance to the work in the crypt at Canterbury. That the earlier bosses at Chichester should show some such resemblance seems natural; the vaulting had to be rebuilt after the fire of 1186–7; the rebuilding of the quire at Canterbury was completed by this time and workmen who had been employed there would have been available.

But when we go to other places where important churches were being built in the years following the rebuilding of Canterbury, although we find keystones richly carved with foliage, the kind of foliage bears little resemblance either to the earlier or the later work at Canterbury. In Southwark Cathedral (324, 325) we find long and deeply cut leaves, some of it rather like seaweed, in New Shoreham trefoil foliage with a strong central midrib, and in St Hugh's quire at Lincoln long straggling trefoil foliage with a very prominent midrib running to the very tip of the leaves. The Lincoln bosses (328–31) are particularly important; we can trace the development of Early English trefoil foliage from St Hugh's quire at the very end of the twelfth century through varying forms; as time goes on we find the leaves becoming shorter, the midrib changes its character, the style of the carving improves and the leaves become more and more the ortho-dox trefoil of Early English foliage sculpture. We have all the stages in the evolution from the high vault of St Hugh's quire, and of the eastern transepts, through the vaulting of the aisles, thence through the western transepts and the nave, to the perfection of the Angel quire in the middle of the thirteenth century.

An intensive study of Early English trefoil foliage would probably prove most illuminating and nowhere can it be studied so satisfactorily as on roof bosses. The shape of the leaves and stem, and particularly the treatment of the midrib, may be important guides to dating. The leaves of fossil plants enable the geologist to trace the succession of strata in which they are found, and somewhat similarly the study of trefoil foliage may be a guide to the relative dates of buildings in various parts of the country. Certainly at Lincoln we get a progressive evolution from perhaps 1180 to 1280.

After Lincoln we have numerous examples of Early English trefoil foliage at Westminster, Salisbury, Worcester, Wells and Ely. In the latter cathedral we can contrast the trefoil foliage in Hugh de Northwold's presbytery of the middle of the thirteenth century with the fourteenth-century work of Alan de Walsingham in the three bays of the quire built after the fall of the central tower (344, 345). At Exeter we can trace foliage sculpture from the very end of the thirteenth century to the middle of the fourteenth. In the quire and chapels of Bristol Cathedral we get examples of pure Decorated foliage (348-51). Following on to still later times we get innumerable examples in cathedral and parish church of the less interesting foliage of the later Gothic period; good examples are to be found in the vaulting of the nave at Winchester, and in the church of St Mary, Redcliffe, while some of the very latest examples are in the priory church of Christchurch, Hampshire.

From the early years of the thirteenth till the beginning of the sixteenth century we find many changes in the treatment of foliage; we can trace these changes in chantries and on capitals, as well as on roof bosses. But the changes in foliage carving during the later period of Gothic architecture need not detain us here; it has been dealt with in many books on architecture.[1] But a word must be said on the interesting fashion at the end of the thirteenth century when the naturalistic style of foliage carving came into being. Whatever we may think of the appropriateness of depicting real plants and flowers on stone carvings, we cannot but be interested and charmed by the extraordinary fidelity to nature that we find. Southwell has achieved a reputation above all other churches for naturalistic foliage owing to the writings of Ruskin, but now that roof bosses can be studied at leisure this pre-eminence is seen to be exaggerated. The Angel quire at Lincoln shows equally faithful copies from nature (336-9), copies that are correct down to minute details, like the

[1] See particularly Samuel Gardner, *English Gothic Foliage Sculpture*.

black tip to hawthorn berries. In the ambulatory at Exeter (340-3), in the quire at Pershore, in the high vault of the transept and the four bays west of the crossing in Westminster Abbey, and in various other places we get equally faithful copies from nature.

The foliage bosses in this style in Westminster Abbey are extremely interesting. A few are found in the transepts and many more in the first four bays west of the crossing. The style must have come in during the building of the Abbey, just after the quire vaulting was finished and while the transepts and the first four bays of the nave were being built. If these were really finished before the death of Henry III in 1272, as maintained by Micklethwaite,[1] we must put back the beginning of naturalistic style in this country to perhaps 1265. It had begun in France earlier still[2] and perhaps its appearance at Westminster was due to the French influence which is found in other ways too in the Abbey, and perhaps it was from Westminster that it spread to other places in England.

In the Angel quire at Lincoln naturalistic foliage is found in profusion. In 1280 the body of St Hugh was translated to the Angel quire, which therefore must have been substantially finished by this date; the bosses are not likely to have been carved later as this would have entailed the re-erection of scaffolding, and we may therefore date them to the few years prior to 1280. They have the appearance of a slightly better technique than those at Westminster, as one might expect from their being perhaps ten years later, when the sculptors at Lincoln had reached a height which was unsurpassed at any later time.

Naturalistic foliage lingered on, though not in profusion, to the end of the Gothic period (352-5). We find examples in the naves of Gloucester and Canterbury, in St Mary, Redcliffe, and even as late as the quire of Christchurch Priory, Hampshire.

The actual plants that can be named with certainty are very varied; we find oak with acorns and leaf galls, maple with its winged seeds, hawthorn with its berries, vine with bunches of grapes, ranunculus, rue, wormwood and many others.

One of the most strange is the yellow water-lily (*Nuphar luteum*), with its unmistakable seed-pods (338). For some reason with which we are unacquainted this plant was a particular favourite; it is found as early as Westminster

---

[1] H. J. Feasey, *Westminster Abbey Historically Described* (with an Account of the Abbey Buildings, by J. T. Micklethwaite), pp. 82, 83.

[2] See Viollet-le-Duc, *Dictionnaire...*, under heading 'Flore'.

Abbey and the Angel quire at Lincoln, and as late as St Mary, Redcliffe, and the west end of the nave at Gloucester.

But while we can name many of the plants represented during the naturalistic period, and even after, there are others which look like natural plants but which we cannot name with certainty. We find also flowers that do not belong to the leaves; some may be real flowers but belonging to other plants, some may be imaginary. At Lincoln for example, we find a wreath of oak leaves with a large flower, rather like a periwinkle in the centre (339).

But foliage was only one way in which roof bosses were ornamented. In the few examples that remain from Norman times heads of men, beasts, or birds are found in greater numbers than foliage patterns, but in early Gothic times the position was reversed and figures are far fewer than foliage sculptures. When figures were first introduced they were very often dragons within and often partly concealed by the foliage. Examples in the quire aisles at Canterbury have already been mentioned; other examples occur in the chapter-house at Salisbury, in the naves of Wells and Gloucester, and in the aisles at Westminster Abbey, and in Blyth Priory (326). Very frequently the dragons are represented eating grapes.

Large figures with foliage playing only a subservient part began to appear early in the thirteenth century. Such figures are decidedly English in style; they are carved out of the actual keystone, not as in France on a flat medallion on the lower surface of the boss. Perhaps some of the earliest examples we have are those in the Lady Chapel and quire at Worcester, which date from about 1224 (284). It is unfortunate that the nineteenth-century restoration of this part of the Cathedral was so very thorough. Few of the figures seem to be quite untouched, and some, such as those in the eastern transepts, seem to be purely nineteenth-century work. Large figures also appear in the transept aisles in Westminster Abbey; some of these are very badly decayed (226), but those in what is now the muniment room are intact and show little weathering, particularly the splendid fight between a centaur and a dragon (230).

In the presbytery at Ely, amid numerous bosses with foliage, there are three figures (85-7), St Etheldreda, the Coronation of the Virgin on the central rib, and in a subordinate position a rather mysterious figure of a monk holding a church in one hand and two keys in the other. The chapter-house at Christ Church, Oxford, has four bosses of about the same period,[1] Christ in Glory, the

---

[1] Illustrated in the *Royal Commission on Historical Monuments, City of Oxford*, Plate 107.

Madonna and Child, St Frideswide, and four lions with a common head. Belonging to a slightly later date are the splendid figures in the aisles of the Angel quire at Lincoln (121-33); to my thinking they surpass all the figures that preceded them, and they were never surpassed by later work. Among them are the Coronation of the Virgin, a Jesse Tree, David and Nathan, a prophet with an apostle, and a queen with two pet dogs. Besides these we get several grotesque figures such as the man and the woman kissing over a vaulting-rib, a naked man fighting with a merman, two wrestlers and a variety of strange and fabulous beasts.

In the fourteenth and fifteenth centuries figure bosses became more and more common. In Exeter (97-104) we have a series beginning about 1300 and going on for fifty years or more. In the ambulatory we see many birds and beasts amid the naturalistic foliage. The four symbols of the evangelists occur in the Lady Chapel and on the high vault of the quire, where also we get a Crucifixion, a Coronation of the Virgin, Samson and the Lion, David and Goliath, and other subjects, with a host of heads of kings, queens, bishops, and perhaps craftsmen. In the later nave we have many more figures, among them Christ in Glory, David, Bishop Grandison, who built the nave, and Canon William de Weston, his right-hand man; both these are very probably portraits. The principal boss in the nave, and one of the finest bosses in the country, shows the murder of St Thomas of Canterbury (Frontispiece), with the kneeling archbishop beside an altar and the four knights in the armour of 1350; Grimm, the cross-bearer, stands on one side. In the same vaulting are numerous heads, one of a queen, perhaps Queen Philippa, and one of a pope, probably John XXII.

Close by Exeter, at Ottery St Mary (170-3), we find Grandison again, but here it is a very conventional figure of a bishop whose contrast to the Exeter boss makes one more than ever suppose that the latter is a portrait. Here, too, is a charming Madonna and Child, St Anne and the Virgin, St John the Baptist, and a Coronation of the Virgin, perhaps one of the best renderings of a subject that was very common on roof bosses.

But the greatest glory of early fourteenth-century roof-sculpture is at Tewkesbury (210-21), where up the centre of the nave are scenes from the life of Our Lord, the Nativity, the Presentation, the Magi in two scenes, the finding in the Temple, the Triumphal Entry, the Last Supper, the Betrayal, the Scourging, the Crucifixion, the Ascension, Pentecost, the Coronation of the Virgin, and Christ in Glory. These bosses vary very much in style and execution, and it seems probable that they were not all carved by the same sculptor, nor even by the same school of sculptors. These are perhaps the earliest examples of storied bosses as distinct from isolated figures, and they are some of the finest examples that have come down to us. The bosses at the sides are angels, carrying instruments of the Passion, censing, and playing a variety of musical instruments. The angels with musical instruments occur also in the slightly later roof at Gloucester (105-12), the idea being probably taken from Tewkesbury.

Storied bosses, apart from isolated scenes, are not common. Norwich is unique in having five series. The earliest is in the south and west walks of the cloisters where we have scenes from the Apocalypse copied, as Dr M. R. James surmised, from an East Anglian manuscript (138-41).[1] Interspersed with these are many more bosses portraying other subjects (142-5). In the east walk most of the bosses are foliage, but towards the north end we come to a series representing the Passion of Our Lord, the Scourging, the Carrying of the Cross, the Crucifixion, the Resurrection, and the Harrowing of Hell; surrounding these are a number of other subjects, human and animal, some grotesques, which have nothing to do with the main series. The scenes from the life of Our Lord are carried on into the north walk, where we find the Sealing of the Tomb, Christ in the garden with St Mary Magdalene, the women at the tomb, Christ on the way to and at the supper at Emmaus, and appearing to the disciples, the incredulity of St Thomas, the Ascension, Pentecost, and some others. These bosses too are surrounded by others with quite unrelated subjects, as in the other walks of the cloisters. The events of Our Lord's life come to an end in the fourth bay; in the fifth bay we get the Coronation of the Virgin, and in the remaining bays a great variety of subjects, some of them scenes from the lives of saints, some grotesques, and some groups of figures to which it is difficult to assign a subject. The eighth bay has a number of bosses representing the story of St Thomas of Canterbury, the murder, burial, translation, and the scourging of Henry II at the shrine.

The cloister bosses at Norwich form undoubtedly the most important series in the country. The cloisters were begun in the last years of the thirteenth century with the east walk, most of which was completed by 1318; the south walk was finished by 1330, and after a pause the west walk was erected between 1338 and 1348. The Black Death seems to have put an end to all work for about fifty years, and the north walk was not begun till early in the fifteenth century.

[1] *The Sculptured Bosses in the Cloisters of Norwich Cathedral.* Norfolk and Norwich Archaeological Society, 1911.

There are nearly 400 bosses in the cloisters,[1] and nearly 100 of these are scenes from the Apocalypse.

The third series of storied bosses at Norwich, in order of date, is in the Bauchon chapel; they date from about 1450, and represent the story of an empress falsely accused, banished, and after going through terrible adventures, finally delivered through the intercession of Our Lady. The story is almost the same as Chaucer's *Man of Law's Tale*.[2]

The fourth series is in the nave where on over 270 bosses are scenes from the Old and the New Testaments (146-65), from the Creation to the Coronation of the Virgin, and on to the general resurrection and the Last Judgement. The roof was erected by Bishop Lyhart who died in 1472.

The fifth series is in the transepts where there are 150 bosses carved from scenes connected with the early life of Our Lord, his birth and childhood and the beginning of his ministry. These bosses are very late, belonging to the beginning of the sixteenth century.

In the cloisters at Worcester we find in the south walk a series of storied bosses representing a Jesse Tree (288-91); at the west end of the walk is Jesse asleep, and going eastward we find on other bosses David and other figures who are no doubt intended for others in the genealogy; the series culminates in the middle of the walk, not with the Nativity as one would expect, but with the Coronation of the Virgin by the Three Persons of the Trinity, represented as three old men. Going to the east end of the same walk we find another series leading up to the same boss of the Coronation, but beginning with the figure of a bishop, asleep like Jesse, and like him with a stem growing out of his body. It has been suggested[3] that this second series represents a spiritual succession or genealogy.

At Nantwich in Cheshire the chancel has a lierne vault with a succession of bosses from east to west in the following order, Christ in Glory, the Coronation of the Virgin, the Annunciation, the Assumption, the Annunciation (a second time), St Anne and the Virgin, the Nativity, the Scourging, the Crucifixion, the Resurrection, 'Noli me tangere'.

---

[1] See an account of the bosses by the Dean of Norwich and Professor E. W. Tristram reprinted from the *Sixth*, *Seventh*, and *Eighth Annual Reports of the Friends of Norwich Cathedral*. The bosses have been cleaned and repainted by Professor Tristram with the best possible results.

[2] See footnote, p. 201.

[3] Canon Wilson, D.D., 'Notes on some of the Bosses in the Cloisters of Worcester Cathedral and in particular on the Jesse Tree in the South Cloister'. *Reports and Papers read at the Meetings of Archaeological Societies*, vol. XXX, part II, p. 578.

At Salle in Norfolk there is a series of wooden bosses in the Chancel (190-3) with scenes from the life of Christ; the Annunciation, the Nativity, the Circumcision, the Epiphany, the Triumphal Entry, the Last Supper, the Crucifixion, the Resurrection, and the Ascension.

With these examples we have practically all the series of storied bosses. But there are endless examples of individual scenes from the Life of Christ, or of Our Lady, besides other historiated bosses which will be noticed later.

The development of the lierne roof increased the number of bosses enormously. In the nave of Norwich, for instance, there are, including foliage bosses, some 350 bosses, whereas if, as in early vaulted roofs, there was only one boss to each bay there would have been but fourteen. But what was gained in quantity was lost in quality, and the later bosses, however interesting they may be, are not usually of the artistic merit of those of earlier times.

Stone bosses form part of the structure of the roof, wooden bosses are merely ornaments. But there are probably far more wooden bosses in the country than stone ones. Amongst the earliest wooden bosses are those in the cloisters at Lincoln and in the nave of Warmington Church, Northamptonshire. In both of these the wooden vaulting is made to resemble a stone vault of the Early English style, with a boss in the centre of every bay, and another between each bay. In later times there is a profusion of wooden bosses. Every type of wooden roof has bosses of this kind. The king-post roofs of the Midlands and the somewhat similar roofs of Somerset have bosses, sometimes large ones, on the middle of the rafters often with figures of angels or men flanking the bosses to east and west;[1] and in the more elaborate roofs of the kind, where the ceiling is filled with panels, there are bosses at each intersection of rafter and purline, but as a rule these subsidiary bosses represent only conventional foliage. Numberless examples occur throughout the country; Market Harborough and Lutterworth are examples of the Midland type, and Bruton and North Cadbury are splendid examples of the Somerset group.

The very low-pitched or nearly flat-panelled roofs are sometimes wonderfully enriched with wooden sculptures; one of the best examples is St Mary, Beverley (17-28), where chancel, nave and aisles are covered with bosses, and here the majority of the carvings are figures of men, beasts, and birds, and comparatively few are merely foliage.

The wooden bosses in the nave at Selby Abbey (194-201) are rather in a class apart; they are square or rectangular with good carvings of a variety of figures

[1] Compare Blythburgh (69).

besides foliage. They survived the fire of 1906 by a curious chance; they were fastened through the roof by wooden pins, and the fire which destroyed the roof burnt the wooden pins, thus letting the bosses fall to the floor before they were burnt, and the greater number were saved and have been replaced.

For the greatest profusion of wooden bosses one must go to the wagon roofs of the West country. These are extremely common in Devon, Somerset, and especially in Cornwall, but they are scarce elsewhere, though a few occur in Wiltshire, Dorsetshire, Hampshire, and elsewhere, including the refectory at Beaulieu Abbey, now used as the parish church, where the bosses are decidedly in the Somerset style and were possibly carved by West-country craftsmen.

These wagon roofs have large wooden bosses at the intersections of the rafters and purlines and so one may get an astonishing number in a single church; at Launceston for instance there are 375 bosses and 30 half-bosses, while even a small village church like St Kew has 193. The carving varies very much. One of the finest of the wagon roofs is that of the refectory at Cleeve Abbey, and though there is nothing but foliage yet it is foliage of an excellent kind. Some of the Somerset wagon roofs have carvings of beasts taken probably from some medieval bestiary. Queen Camel is the best of these, but Old Cleeve, St Decuman's, Sampford Brett, and Wootton Courtenay have carvings in exactly the same style. Besides these beasts there are various other figures which are common to two or more churches with wagon roofs. There is a certain type of head found at Dunster and Luccombe; two dragons with intertwined necks are common to Dunster and St Decuman's, and birds with necks similarly intertwined occur at Stoodleigh. Three rabbits with only three ears between them are found at various churches in Devonshire, especially round Dartmoor.

The roof bosses in Cornwall have a certain family likeness, which is shared by examples from west Devon; there are a variety of foliage patterns, and also a spiral ornament which can be traced from church to church throughout the county. It is common in Cornwall to find nearly all the bosses in a church of foliage patterns with the exception of a very few with Passion emblems; at St Austell amongst the very numerous foliage bosses there is one with scourges; at Fowey, out of the 157 bosses, all are foliage except three, two bearing a heart encircled with the Crown of Thorns, and one bearing a small cross in the centre of foliage. On the whole, the Cornish bosses are poor and are in marked contrast to the wonderfully carved bench ends which are such a feature of the county.

Many of the later bosses in the West-country roofs have four leaves projecting

out into the angles between rafters and purlines and on the actual intersection
is a small square, or other shaped figure carved either with foliage or with
Passion emblems or with heads or figures; examples are to be found in the
south aisle at Selworthy, the nave at Shepton Mallet, and the nave at Banwell.
The same kind of boss, with what one may call angle foliage, is found on the
panelling of the Somerset low-pitched king-post roofs, and the best examples
produce an effect of great richness. Nor is this type confined to the West
country, but may be found in many places on rich timber roofs, as in the south
transept at Ely and formerly in the church of the Holy Trinity at Coventry.
Sometimes the spreading leaves extend outward along the rafters and purlines
instead of over the angles between them; in the Ely examples they extend in all
eight directions. This spreading arrangement of leaves from a boss is usually
only to be found in wooden bosses, though in France one sometimes sees something of the same kind in stone where the sculpture has been keyed onto the
keystone after the latter has been put in place.

Some of the West-country bosses are peculiar and have no counterpart in
other churches, for instance, the rectangular bosses with figures of saints in the
nave at Selworthy, the Coronation of the Virgin at Buckland Monachorum also
on a rectangular boss. No doubt many more curious examples remain to be
discovered among the wagon roofs of the three south-western counties.

Though they will be noted again later a word must be said here about the
very curious motif which appears over and over again amongst all classes of roof
bosses, stone and wood, from Norman times to the very end of the Gothic
period. This is the face or head with leafy stems growing out of the mouth, or
sometimes out of the eyes, ears, and nose, or out of the forehead (300-19). The
device is too definite and too ubiquitous to be merely the fancy of the artist;
some meaning it must have had, though what it was is a matter of surmise.
It may possibly be connected with tree-worship, and the motif may have been
handed down from pre-Christian times, a fertility figure connected with the
success of the harvest.

And perhaps connected with such things are the female fertility figures known
to Irish antiquaries by the name of 'sheila-na-gig', now usually called sheilas
simply. They too must have come down from remote times before the intro-
duction of Christianity. These figures are by no means confined to Ireland;
quite a number occur in English churches, and many more once existed, but
have been removed by those whose sense of decorum outweighed their interest

in archaeology. Probably the best known of these figures is the Norman corbel on the outside of the chancel of Kilpeck Church, Herefordshire. Among actual roof bosses I have found only a few sheilas; there is one at South Tawton, Devon; one in the nave of St Mary, Redcliffe; and two in the west walk of the cloisters at Wells Cathedral. There are also a certain number of female figures which, though not actually sheilas, seem to have some relation to them. There are also a number of phallic figures. These are sometimes found on bosses over or near to nave windows; in such situations they occur in the naves of Winchester, Worcester, and St Mary, Redcliffe.

There are too a certain number of bosses which are frankly coarse; amongst others are a few carvings of men at stool; the best example is under the tower of St Mary, Redcliffe (42). It is a curious commentary on the mentality of these medieval carvers to find such a subject, and another even more coarse, in close juxtaposititon to a representation of the five wounds of Our Lord, and to the arms of Our Lady; yet such things were not unusual in the later Middle Ages, though they are nowhere, perhaps, more in evidence than here, under the tower, and in the high vault of the nave of St Mary, Redcliffe.

Heraldic bosses appear early in the fourteenth century, and in the fifteenth they become more and more common. In the nave of Exeter dating from the middle of the fourteenth century there are a fair number of heraldic bosses. In the nave of Canterbury (65-8), of the early part of the fifteenth century, there are many, and in the north transept and more particularly in the cloisters the heraldic ornamentation of the bosses becomes profuse. In St George's Chapel, Windsor (272-9), there is a gorgeous display of royal heraldry, and the wooden roof of the quire at Winchester (239-54) is decorated with large wooden shields with coats of arms, and Passion emblems treated heraldically; these shields are bolted onto a somewhat earlier roof; it looks as though Bishop Fox wanted to have a lierne roof as at Windsor, but as the walls would not have stood a stone vault he had to do his best with wooden bosses. Another fine heraldic series is to be found in the Divinity School at Oxford.[1]

There is an extremely fine series of wooden heraldic bosses in St Machar's Cathedral, Aberdeen (9-12), the roof of which was built by Bishop Dunbar about 1520. The bosses are arranged in three rows, the first boss in the central

---

[1] The bosses are fully described by the late Sir William St John Hope in 'The Heraldry and Sculptures of the Vault of the Divinity School at Oxford', *Archaeological Journal*, vol. LXXI, no. 283; 2nd ser., vol. XXI, no. 3, pp. 217–60.

row bears the Medici arms of Pope Leo X (1513–21); this is followed by the personal arms of two archbishops and eleven bishops of Scottish sees, including Dunbar, and ends with the arms of the Prior of St Andrew's and of the University of Aberdeen; the row to the north has the arms of the Empire followed by those of various European countries, and ends with those of King's College, Aberdeen; the row to the south commences with the arms of Scotland, followed by those of the Confessor and of various noble Scottish families, ending with the town of Aberdeen. This is an outstanding heraldic series, and is in a very good state of preservation; the painting must be modern.

At Godalming there is a series of early sixteenth-century wooden bosses with coats of arms, including those of Fox, bishop of Winchester, surrounded by the garter, and the Howard arms without the Flodden augmentation, which would seem to date the bosses between the year 1500 when Fox became bishop of Winchester, and 1513 the date of the battle of Flodden.[1] There are some examples of arms being impaled which should be quarterly, among them France and England.

Many churches show local characteristics in the carving of their roof bosses. On the other hand there are many places, sometimes quite far apart, where one feels that the same craftsmen were responsible for the bosses. In early times the combination of dragons and trefoil foliage is widespread, and examples from many places show a great family likeness, so that it seems that some of this work may have been done by craftsmen who went from one place to another. At Gloucester, however, the monks themselves built the vaulting of the nave in 1242; this must have been very exceptional as seems to be implied in the Gloucester cartulary.[2] But the roof bosses with their dragons and trefoil foliage are so akin to what we find in other places and are of such high artistic merit that it is difficult to suppose that they were carved by any but highly skilled craftsmen. May not the monks who built the vaulting with their own hands have employed craftsmen to carve the bosses? Or perhaps some master-builder may have become a monk in the monastery.

Almost everywhere there are little local characteristics, a general feeling, that makes the carving in one cathedral or great church slightly different from

[1] The date may be narrowed down still more; the Prince of Wales's feathers appear on several bosses; after Henry VIII came to the throne in 1509 there was no Prince of Wales for 101 years.

[2] 'Et anno Domini millesimo ducentesimo quadragesimo secundo completa est nova volta in navi ecclesiae, non auxilio fabrorum ut primo, sed animosa virtute monachorum item in ipso loco existentium.' Historia et cartularium Monasterii Sancti Petri Gloucestriae. Edited by W. H. Hart (Rolls Series), vol. 1, p. 29.

that in others, and there are some churches where the style is completely different from what is found anywhere else.

At Lincoln there is something distinctive about the bosses, foliage as well as figures, which mark them off from those in other places; and it is understandable that in such a great church, which must have been under construction almost continuously for the best part of a hundred years, a local school of sculptors should have grown up and that they should have developed a local style.[1]

The case of Tewkesbury is interesting; there are fifteen large bosses up the nave dealing with the Life of Christ from the Nativity to Christ in Glory (210-17). It has always seemed to me that more than one set of craftsmen were concerned in their production. There are five bosses on each of which a large number of figures are represented, the Triumphal Entry, the Last Supper, the Betrayal, the Ascension and Pentecost. The Ascension and Pentecost seem to me to have been carved by master hands and the other three by less experienced craftsmen who had no doubt learned their craft from the masters; the three bosses in question seem to me to lack some of the extreme delicacy of the other two. In the ten bosses with the larger figures it seems to me unlikely that the very crude bosses of the angel guiding the Magi and of the Scourging could have been carved by the same hands that were responsible for the Crucifixion, the Coronation of the Virgin and Christ in Glory. I do not wish to lay too much stress on these points, but it does look as though more than one set of craftsmen were concerned in the carving of these bosses.

One of the most marked examples of a local style is seen on the roof bosses in the Lady Chapel at Ely (89-96). The short stumpy figures, many of them demi-figures, are quite unlike anything that occurs in the Cathedral itself or elsewhere. The heads, of which there are a great number, are also distinctive.

Distinctive too are the heads in the nave at Canterbury whether of men and women or of beasts (61-4); so too are the double heads, sometimes with only three eyes between them, and the double, triple, or quadruple heads of beasts arranged round a central hole. The way too that the vaulting-ribs are made to appear to run into the human heads or into the mouths of beasts is quite peculiar to Canterbury among existing bosses.

The bosses in the high vault of the nave at Winchester are unlike any others; it is true that there are a number of heraldic bosses which are not peculiar, but the foliage bosses cannot be matched elsewhere; the foliage is very conventional

[1] For a full account of the roof bosses at Lincoln see *Archaeologia*, vol. LXXXV, pp. 23 ff.

and not very interesting, except in so far as it is peculiar to Winchester; a few small heads in the centre of some of the foliage bosses are also peculiar.

The very small and late perpendicular bosses on the fan-vaulting at Sherborne Abbey are also in a class by themselves (202-9). We find many of the usual subjects, a mermaid, birds eating grapes, a pelican feeding its young, St Michael and the Dragon, but they are in a distinctive style and seem to me to differ from late bosses found anywhere else; and among them there are unusual subjects, such as that of a man with a crossbow aiming at the rump of another man, possibly an allusion to quarrels that broke out between the monks and the townspeople.

When we come to wooden bosses, especially those on the wagon roofs of the West country, we find that the same patterns, whether of conventional foliage or of other subjects, are found in many places. For instance at Morwenstowe in Cornwall and at Lifton in Devon we find a double-headed eagle, a pelican feeding its young, and a head with long hair hanging down at the side, which are so much alike that they must have been carved by the same carvers. Of course many of these wooden bosses may have been shop-produced, have been made in some centre and sent to places where they were wanted, for unlike stone bosses, wooden bosses would almost certainly have been carved in the workshop and not after they were put up. But not by any means all of these wooden bosses have indications that they were shop-produced; in many places we get bosses so peculiar in style that they were in all probability carved by local men. At Congresbury, for example, there is a set of wooden bosses very unlike any others that have come to light (73-6); there are a number of heads in slightly cusped borders, mostly with conventional foliage round them; there are also some geometrical patterns that are unusual; though the heads are not specially well carved, yet the whole lay-out of these bosses shows considerable skill.

At King's Nympton (115, 116) there are some curious and very crude heads, six of men and two of women; the men are all grotesque, and have mouth foliage, and they and the women seem to be peculiar to this church.

At Stoodleigh (294) there are no less than four mermaids, each holding a comb and mirror; but their design is hopeless; they look like a child's attempt at portraying a mermaid; there are also two bosses each with two dragons with necks intertwined, a design which occurs in other places in the West country, but here again the design is extremely crude; there are also a number of heads which are almost as childlike in their execution. It looks as though some local and inexperienced man had tried his hand at these carvings and had not made a success of it.

A really intensive study of the bosses on wagon roofs, especially of those in Cornwall, would probably reveal a number of fairly well-carved bosses made very likely at some one place by moderately experienced hands, and many crude and badly executed examples which were probably carved by local men of small experience, and in some churches one might find a mixture of the two.

At St Just-in-Roseland (113, 114) there are roof bosses which are unique in my experience. They are square flat bosses that have designs painted on their flat lower faces. It is possible that the painting is not medieval, but Professor Tristram, to whom I showed the photographs, is of opinion that it is. There is no local tradition of their having been painted within the memory of old inhabitants, and their present state suggests that they cannot have been painted for a long time. Most of the subjects suggest medieval work; there are a number of Passion emblems of the kind found in the late fifteenth or early sixteenth century, but there are others that are unusual, for instance a seven-branched candlestick; a phœnix; ☧ flanked by A and Ω; an anchor; three fish *hurient in fesse* and above them the word ΙΧΘΥΣ. Greek lettering is practically unknown on roof bosses[1] and this might be held to indicate a very late or even modern date; but on the whole of the evidence I am inclined to date these bosses as very late medieval examples.

The study of roof bosses and of English medieval sculpture in general is rather like the study of evolution from fossil remains; in both there are so many gaps in the record. The greater number of the monastic churches, great and small, are lost to us; if only half what has been destroyed had remained, we might have obtained a much more connected view of English roof bosses than we actually possess.

The style of carving the whole keystone, often with very deeply cut designs, was peculiarly English. In France in early times the style was for the lower surface of the boss to consist of a flat plaque with rather shallow carving. In Durham two bosses in the quire, the Agnus Dei and Abraham (81, 82), are typically French in style. In France one finds endless examples of such flat plaques, and some may be studied at close quarters in the museum at the Abbey of Jumièges.

Very often the lower side of the boss was left uncarved as a flat surface with a hole in the centre (356). With such a boss it was possible at any subsequent date to fit on a carving, often of wood. The boss of Christ sitting between two

---

[1] The only other example I know is at Spreyton where there are two bosses, one with A and Ω, the other with ☧, but they are almost certainly modern.

candlesticks in the apse at Amiens is a wooden boss of this kind. It is obvious that such carvings may be considerably later than the vaulting to which they are attached. A boss in the nave at Coutances is an extreme example; field-glasses reveal lettering on it, but it needs a photograph to see that the inscription records that the carving was made by 'Aime Doublet age de 18 ans en 1810'. It often happened that no carving was ever placed on the boss, and such bosses with plain unornamented lower surfaces remain in very many French churches.

By the middle of the fifteenth century roof bosses in France were beginning to lose their simplicity and to show exaggerations in various directions. One of the new forms took the shape of large circular or polygonal plates, often with long finials, and generally with open tracery work in the middle (358); they are much larger in diameter than the actual keystone, and could not possibly have formed an original part of it. Viollet-le-Duc[1] says that some of them are of such delicacy that they remind one of metal rather than of stone-work. He explains how such structures are fastened to the keystone by a hook and a metal bar.

Another exaggeration that appeared in France was the development of pendant bosses. We get a few such in late roofs in England, in Henry VII's Chapel, Westminster, for instance (231, 233-4), and in the wooden roof at St David's. In France they are found in abundance in many churches large and small (364-7). They sometimes resemble inverted pinnacles or even towers, and they tend to become extremely elaborate. They also must have been fixed on after the building of the vault, and since some of them must be extremely heavy they must be supported by means of metal rods or chains. In the church of St Gervais at Falaise there was part of a pendant boss, the lower part of which had been broken off, and on the under-surface of the remaining part were two links of a chain, showing that the pendant must have been supported by such means.

In England it is rare to find Renaissance details on roof bosses; the Renaissance came later to England than it did to France, and in England the Reformation put a somewhat abrupt end to the production of roof bosses except in a few exceptional cases. But in France the production of roof bosses was still going on when Renaissance art reached the country. There are some very good examples in the Cathedral at Evreux in carvings, probably of wood, keyed onto flat stone bosses as described above; some of them are pure Renaissance without any trace of Gothic art (359).

[1] *Dictionnaire...*, vol. III, p. 272.

CHAPTER II

THE TRINITY AND THE LIFE OF CHRIST

THE MAJORITY of figure bosses, apart from mere heads, are religious subjects, and may be classified under various headings, e.g. the Trinity, scenes from the Life of Christ, Our Lady and scenes from her life, saints, angels, symbols of the evangelists, emblems of the Passion, etc.

THE TRINITY. This was, of course, a very common subject of medieval carving and painting, but by far the greater number of such representations must have been destroyed in the sixteenth and the seventeenth centuries. In roof bosses, however, a considerable number remain.

The commonest representation consists of a figure of God the Father, usually represented as an aged man, holding a crucifix before him; sometimes, but not always, the Holy Ghost is represented as a dove. Émile Mâle maintains[1] that this figure was intended to show that the Father was associated with the Passion of the Son. There is a late thirteenth-century example in the Lady Chapel at Chester (71); here the Father, bearded and crowned, is represented as a middle-aged man holding the crucifix in his two hands; on one arm of the cross the Dove is perched and leans over towards the head of the dead Christ; on either side is a censing angel with outspread wings. A rather later example at Lichfield (118) shows the Father as an aged man; one hand is on the Cross, the other is raised in benediction; no trace of the Dove can be seen, but the boss is much worn or mutilated. In the porch of the church of St John the Baptist at Peterborough is a still later example; here also the Father is an old man and the Dove is not visible, but here again the boss is much weathered; there are four censing angels around.

Other examples with no Dove are at Selworthy, under the tower at St Andrew, Worcester, and in the quire at Melrose Abbey. In the quire at Norwich and in the nave of St Mary, Redcliffe, it is not quite clear whether the Dove was meant to be represented or not.

There is an extremely curious example in the west porch of the Cathedral at Peterborough (180), where the Father is shown with a beardless face surrounded

[1] *L'Art Religieux de la Fin du Moyen Âge*, p. 140.

by rays, the same sort of face as appears again and again in roof bosses, to which I have given the name of a 'sun face'; the right hand is raised in benediction and the left hand holds aloft the left hand of the Son; the latter is a demi-figure only and is represented naked to the waist, wearing the Crown of Thorns, the right hand held to the breast and the stigmata on the hands well marked; in fact the figure is not really Christ on the Cross but the Image of Pity. Above and at the side is the Dove apparently speaking into the ear of the Father; on each side, amid indications of clouds, is the demi-figure of an angel. It is interesting to compare this very strange composition with the example from Chester and it would be interesting to know the reasons for this change of symbolism, how the Father came to acquire the 'sun face', and how the Crucifix became the Image of Pity.

Another form of symbolizing the Trinity was under the form of three old men. There is a fourteenth-century example in the cloisters at Worcester (288) where the three Persons are crowning the Virgin; as far as can be seen in the present worn state of the boss there is no difference between the three figures. Norwich has a late fifteenth-century example in the nave (165); the three Persons are seated, each is bearded, each has a hand raised in blessing; rays proceed from behind Father and Son; the Father and the Holy Ghost wear crowns, the Son a Crown of Thorns. Among the late wooden bosses in the quire at Peterborough the Trinity is represented as three men standing; the central one, the Father, is crowned, has the right hand raised in benediction, and in the left hand carries a large orb; on the right is a similar bearded figure, but not crowned, for the Son, and on the left the Holy Ghost shown as a young, beardless man.

In the Divinity School at Oxford there are demi-figures of the Father and the Son, the Father with a crown, the Son with the Crown of Thorns, and showing the stigmata, and standing on their shoulders is the Dove with its wings outspread behind the heads of the other two figures.

On a boss just over the east window of St George's Chapel, Windsor, there is an unusual representation of the Trinity (272); on the right is the Father, a seated figure of an old man; on the left also seated is the Son, a younger man with his robe open to the waist to show the wound in his side. Both figures place their hands on a large clasped book which lies horizontally between them; above the book is the Dove with spreading wings, and below the book is the orb surmounted by a cross, and divided into the three traditional parts, the lower half ornamented by wavy lines to represent the ocean, the upper half divided by a vertical line to represent Europe and Asia.

In the south transept of St Mary, Redcliffe (33-5), the Three Persons are represented by heads and a demi-figure on three separate bosses, one in the centre of each bay. The one to the north is evidently meant for the Father; the head, surrounded by the cross-bearing nimbus, is that of an aged man, with long hair and beard, and a puckered brow; it is extremely well chiselled. The next boss is a demi-figure surrounded by conventional clouds; the figure wears a crown, is bearded and has both hands raised with all the fingers extended; the stigmata in the hands and the wound in the side are quite plainly shown. In fact, the Son is here shown as the Image of Pity, but wearing a crown instead of the Crown of Thorns. The third boss shows the head of an old man with long hair and beard, and though it bears no nimbus it must, it seems, be taken to represent the Third Person of the Trinity owing to its position in relation to the bosses representing the First and Second Persons. There are only three bays in the transept; in the centre of the first is the Father, in the centre of the second the Son, and the head of an aged man with long hair and beard in the centre of the third bay can only be meant for the Holy Ghost. I have laid stress on this point for a peculiar reason; in the long hair at the side and on the beard below the face are four small figures; two seem to be lions, one is a smooth animal with a rather human head, such as occurs in several other places in the vaulting, and the fourth is a grinning human face with a protruding tongue. It is difficult to know why such figures, one of them definitely grotesque, should be thus represented hidden in the hair and beard of the figure of the Holy Ghost. Hidden they certainly are, for they entirely escape notice as seen from the floor below; I doubt whether field-glasses would show them unless one knew from photographs that they were there. I almost feel that they were put there by some craftsman in a spirit of mischief, if not even in a spirit of actual disrespect for images which, in a slightly later period, led to outbreaks of iconoclasm.

God the Father is rarely depicted alone, the Holy Ghost never as far as roof bosses are concerned. It is not always possible to distinguish between the Father and the Son. An aged figure with a cross-bearing nimbus may quite well represent the Son. But there are a few cases where it is possible to say that the Father is intended. One of these is in the quire at Peterborough, where a crowned figure carrying an orb is so exactly like the Father in the Trinity boss close by that it must be meant for the same.

FIGURES OF CHRIST. Single figures or heads of Our Lord, apart from scenes from his life, are extremely common. There is an early example in the chapter-house at Christ Church, Oxford, where Our Lord blesses with the right hand and holds a book in the left. Another thirteenth-century example is in the south aisle of the nave at Lincoln; here is a demi-figure with a hand raised in blessing; in the cloisters of the same Cathedral there is a seated figure of Christ.

In the nave of Tewkesbury there is a fine figure of Christ[1] of the early part of the fourteenth century; it is the culminating point of the scenes from the life of Our Lord which are found on the bosses up the central rib in the nave. In Gloucester there is a slightly later figure also surrounded by angels on other bosses. In the nave at Exeter there is a figure without a nimbus which probably represents Our Lord; one hand is raised in blessing, the other holds a book; the robe is draped so that the left side is bare, probably to show the wound in the side though this is not now definitely visible; the date of this figure is about the middle of the fourteenth century. At Ottery St Mary is a boss of about the same date showing Christ as a young man, with a short beard, holding in his left hand an orb surmounted by a cross. In the Lady Chapel at Ely there is a head of Our Lord wearing the Crown of Thorns, also a demi-figure blessing and holding open the tunic to show the wound in the side; the stigmata on the hands are plainly shown.

Of a still later date is a demi-figure in the south porch at Gloucester; Our Lord holds up both hands on which are the stigmata and the wound in the side is also shown; on other bosses adoring angels surround Christ.

Besides individual figures of Christ there are numerous scenes from his life in which he is depicted. These are very numerous and only a short summary can be given here.

THE NATIVITY. I know only seven examples of this scene, perhaps the best is the early fourteenth-century example which commences the great series at Tewkesbury (210); Our Lady is shown lying on a bed, and above her is the Child in swaddling clothes lying in a manger; over the manger are the heads of the ox and the ass; at the foot of the bed, with a restored head, St Joseph stands

[1] I gave this as God the Father in *Archaeologia*, vol. LXXIX, p. 83, and Plate XXX, fig. 4, but it was pointed out to me by the Rev. E. G. Benson that the figure is flanked by angels with Passion emblems and it is therefore almost certainly meant for Our Lord.

leaning on a staff, and on the other side of the boss is an angel. In the north aisle of the nave at Worcester is another example (286) with a very similar arrangement of figures, but behind Our Lady's head is the figure of a woman, doubtless the midwife; Our Lady stretches one arm up to the Child in the manger. In the nave at Norwich (159) Our Lady is seated on one side and St Joseph on the other; between them the Child, with a nimbus, is lying naked in the manger. In the transepts at Norwich there are several examples dating from the beginning of the sixteenth century. At Nantwich is a curious Nativity; Our Lady is sitting on a couch with St Joseph at the foot; above is the manger; the ox and the ass are holding the ends of a cloth in their mouths, and in it they are lowering down the Child to his mother, who holds out her hands to receive him. In St Helen, Norwich (166), the Child has apparently just had a bath, and a woman attendant is handing him to his mother, who holds a large towel. I do not know this subject elsewhere in England, but it occurs in France, and I have seen it on wall-paintings in Greek churches in Cyprus.

The earlier representations of the Nativity are all of the type in which Our Lady is shown lying on a bed. But a second form of the Nativity in art began in Italy towards the end of the fourteenth century. It owed its origin to the 'Revelations' of St Bridget of Sweden (1303–73), who describes how Our Lady knelt in a cave in an ecstasy, when, suddenly, the Child was lying before her radiating an ineffable light. All readers will be familiar with this new rendering; it rapidly spread from Italy and very soon all but took the place of the old. The latter did survive, but in a very subordinate place, till the end of the Gothic period. On roof bosses in this country, however, there is only one example, so far recorded, of the new rendering, and that is in the north transept at Norwich where the boss is divided into three compartments; in the centre the Child lies on the ground before his mother while rays of light come from above; in the right-hand compartment is St Joseph, and in the left the ox and the ass.

THE PRESENTATION IN THE TEMPLE. One of the scenes at Tewkesbury is probably meant for the Presentation; Our Lady, holding the Child in her arms, stands amid three other figures, two men, one a woman; one of the men holds a bowl or basket in one hand; the subject is not quite clear, but coming as it does just after the Nativity in the series it is probably the Presentation. There is another example in the nave at Norwich and several in the transepts.

THE CIRCUMCISION. This subject is not always very easy to distinguish from the last, but there are a few examples which are unmistakable. There is one in the north transept at Norwich in which the high priest holds a knife in his hand, which makes the subject certain. Another good example is at Salle in Norfolk (191); here Our Lady, seated, holds the Child on her knee, and sitting opposite to her is the high priest with a knife in one hand; Our Lady is giving the Child her breast to distract his attention; three other figures are depicted, one probably intended for St Joseph. Almost exactly the same rendering of the subject is to be seen in stained glass at St Peter Mancroft, Norwich.

THE SHEPHERDS AT BETHLEHEM. It is only at Norwich and Salle that this subject is found on roof bosses. At Salle there is a very good wooden boss of the shepherds at Bethlehem (190). Our Lady is seated holding the Child on her knee; facing her is St Joseph and behind him are the three shepherds, one of whom is playing a pipe; behind the figures is a very high manger with cattle food in it, and one of the beasts is shown eating from it. In the nave at Norwich the shepherds are depicted on several bosses, but the actual scene at Bethlehem is not shown. But in the north transept there are nine bosses connected with the subject. In two of them the angels are appearing to the shepherds; in another the three shepherds are seen on their journey, the first one playing on a musical instrument; in another the three shepherds are before the door of a house and one of them is playing the bagpipes. In the central scene one shepherd is kneeling before Our Lady who is holding the naked Child on her knee; the other two shepherds are standing and touching their hats; St Joseph is leaning on his staff, and behind is a thatched gable of a house with a pointed star on it, and two beasts can be seen within the building.

THE EPIPHANY. At Tewkesbury there are two bosses of the Magi, in one they are seen on their journey, with an angel urging them on from behind and with a star in front of them; in the other (211) one of the Magi kneels before Our Lady and Child, while two stand behind; over the Child is a large star. In the nave at Norwich the central scene is not shown, but on several bosses the Magi are seen with their gifts. In the transepts the scene appears on nine bosses; the Magi are seen on their journey, sometimes on horseback; at Bethlehem the scene is much like the one with the shepherds, one is kneeling and two are standing and there is the thatched roof with a star on it. In all these delineations of the Magi one of them is shown as an old man, one middle aged, and one a young man.

THE MASSACRE OF THE INNOCENTS. In the nave of Norwich, Herod is seen speaking to two soldiers with drawn swords, and on two other bosses are very realistic sculptures of soldiers piercing naked children with swords. In the transepts the subject is considerably amplified; Herod appears on a number of bosses; he inquires of the Magi, charges them to return, consults the chief priests and scribes, is 'exceeding wrath', and he gives orders for the slaughter. A soldier is shown dismembering a child, and another has a naked child thrown over his shoulder, while two women stand by in attitudes of grief. Finally, the souls of the Innocents are depicted as three naked children standing with their hands joined while seven angels conduct them to heaven; one angel is playing on a lute.

THE FLIGHT INTO EGYPT. In the nave at Norwich, Our Lady seated on an ass carries the Child, in swaddling clothes, in her arms. In the transepts there are a number of bosses dealing with this subject. An angel speaking to St Joseph occurs several times; Our Lady comes out of a door carrying the Child and St Joseph takes her by the hand, and there are a number of representations of the actual flight. There is an unusual scene of the arrival in Egypt; in the background Our Lady can be seen on the ass; in front St Joseph speaks to a young man, and at the side is a seated figure in a striking headdress, probably intended for Pharaoh, while in the background is a house. Finally comes the scene when the angel tells St Joseph that Herod is dead. The death of Herod occupies two bosses; in one Herod is lying on a bed; his soul is coming out of his mouth and is being seized by one of three demons who stand beside the bed; in the other Herod is lying dead and his friends stand beside him weeping.

THE FINDING IN THE TEMPLE AND CHRIST AMONG THE DOCTORS. At Tewkesbury is a boss of Our Lady seated and stretching her arms out and holding the hands of the Child, who stands on a seat before her; the scene is perhaps not quite clear, but I have attributed it to the Finding.[1] In the nave at Norwich, Our Lady on one boss and St Joseph on another are probably meant to

---

[1] *Archaeologia*, vol. LXXIX, p. 80.

be seeking for the Child, and on another the Child Christ is seen seated amid the doctors who carry books, and wear tippets edged with ermine. In the transepts are many scenes connected with this subject; in one Christ is seated in a high-backed chair with a book in his hand, and round him are four doctors, also with books and ermine tippets; in another Our Lady and St Joseph appear on one side, and on yet another they appear to be leading the Child away.

THE BAPTISM IN THE JORDAN. This subject occurs in the nave at Norwich; Our Lord stands naked in the waters which cover him up to the waist, while St John the Baptist pours water on him out of a huge vase; on two other bosses close by angels are shown taking charge of Christ's garments. In the transepts are two bosses of the subject; in both Our Lord stands in the water up to his knees, while St John the Baptist on dry land empties a vase of water over him. On one of the bosses a very small figure of God the Father is seen in a cloud, and just below is the Dove.

THE TEMPTATION. This is found on a late boss in the quire at Peterborough, where the Devil appears as a very strange figure with a second face on his belly; one leg is flexed at the knee and a wooden stump is strapped onto it; in his hand he holds a stone. Apart from this I know of no example of this subject except in the nave and transepts at Norwich. In the nave a very grotesque figure holds a number of stones; in the transept one example shows the Devil with a second face on his belly; in another he holds a stone; and in yet another he and Christ are seen on the pinnacle of the temple.

THE LIFE OF CHRIST BEFORE THE PASSION. Various scenes are to be found at Norwich, a few in the nave, many in the transepts, and nowhere else as far as I know. In the nave is the Marriage Feast at Cana, with only two figures at the table, Christ and the Virgin; but the scene is recognized by the fact that on the ground in front of the table are three large vessels with hinged covers; on another boss the vessels are seen being filled, and another shows them standing on a table beside which is the Governor of the feast. In the transepts there are a number of feasts, one of which, at least, is the Marriage Feast, as can be seen from the figure pouring water into a flagon; this scene is more elaborate than the one in the nave, for twelve figures are shown. The

Supper at Bethany can be recognized in the nave at Norwich by the prone figure of St Mary Magdalene in front of the table.

In the transepts at Norwich we find among other scenes Christ with St John the Baptist; Christ healing the sick, one of whom is being brought to him in a wheelbarrow; Christ casting out devils, preaching the Sermon on the Mount, preaching in the Temple, calling the apostles, asleep in the ship, preaching from the ship, in the house of Peter's wife's mother.

It is curious that some of these scenes are not more often found on roof bosses, and that it should have been left for carvers very nearly at the end of the Gothic period to portray them.

We now come to the subjects connected with the Passion of Christ and these, unlike the earlier scenes, are to be found in a number of places; the Crucifixion naturally preponderates.

THE TRIUMPHAL ENTRY. The earliest example is to be found in the Tewkesbury (212) series, where Our Lord rides on an ass towards a gateway with flanking turrets; from a window over the door a figure casts out a garment; under the ass's feet are traces of palm branches. In the nave at Norwich there is only the single figure of Christ riding on an ass; the head is broken; the ass has a halter, not a bridle. On some neighbouring bosses are figures which are probably meant for the multitude attending. But the finest carving of this subject is on a wooden boss at Salle (192); Our Lord rides on an ass, which again has a halter and not a bridle; he rides towards a high gateway with small turrets on the top, and on the turrets stand two figures with some objects in their hands which they seem about to throw down. Behind Christ are four apostles and two other figures in front probably typify the crowd. Some of the faces are extraordinarily well carved.

THE LAST SUPPER. The earliest example, that at Tewkesbury, shows Our Lord seated at a table with Our Lady and eight apostles; St John has his head resting on the table in front of Christ; on the near side of the table is Judas, kneeling with a large salt in one hand and with the other hand resting on a dish on the table; above are two censing angels. At Salle eleven apostles are shown; four being seated on the near side of the table; St John is leaning forward in front of Our Lord. In the nave at Norwich there are seven apostles and Our Lady; St John is leaning forward and Our Lord has one arm over his neck. This example is peculiar in that one is supposed to be looking down on the table from above; one apostle seems to be holding a bottle, another a chalice; on the table are a loaf and a dish with two fish in it; an apostle has a large knife in his hand.

THE AGONY IN THE GARDEN. This scene occurs only in the nave at Norwich; Our Lord is kneeling and in front of him is the chalice and host; this is, of course, an incorrect rendering; the host should not appear, for the chalice of the Agony is not the chalice of the Last Supper. On other bosses near the above are figures representing apostles.

THE BETRAYAL. This is well represented at Tewkesbury (213); in the centre of the boss Judas kisses Christ; behind him are three soldiers in armour; one, whose whole figure is visible, has a surcoat over his armour, a sword in its scabbard, and a small round shield with a central boss; on his helmet is a fan-crest of a kind found on seals of about 1300; behind the soldiers is a man carrying a lantern; on the other side are seven apostles with St Peter in the foreground severing the ear of Malchus towards whom Our Lord extends his hand. In the nave at Norwich Judas kisses Christ and soldiers in armour are indicated at one side; one of them can be seen to be wearing plate armour of the type of the latter part of the fifteenth century. St Peter and Malchus are represented on a separate boss, and it is the left ear of Malchus that is being severed.

CHRIST BEFORE PILATE, THE CROWNING WITH THORNS, THE MOCKING. These subjects are found in the nave at Norwich only. In the first scene Pilate is seated in a high-backed chair with a canopy; Christ stands before him with several other figures round. In the Crowning with Thorns two figures have each a thick stem in their hands which they are twisting round and presumably meant by so doing to split the stems to form the crown; this rendering of the subject is found also on wood-carving of late fifteenth or early sixteenth century. In the Mocking scene Christ is seated in a chair and is blindfolded, with two mocking figures on each side, one of them has his tongue out.

THE SCOURGING. At Tewkesbury Our Lord stands behind a tall stake round which his hands are bound, while two tormentors stand on either side;

the boss is much worn, but even in its pristine state it must have been rather crude. In the east walk of the cloisters at Norwich there is another example which may be slightly earlier than that at Tewkesbury, but it is somewhat damaged. The example from Nantwich is much later; here again Christ is fastened by his arms to a high post, while two tormentors scourge him; one holds knotted cords, the other a birch rod.

THE CARRYING OF THE CROSS. The only example is in the east walk of the cloisters at Norwich; Christ has the cross over his shoulders and another figure following carries the three nails in his hand; this is an early example of a Passion emblem, if it can be so classed; it probably dates from early in the fourteenth century.

THE NAILING TO THE CROSS. One example only of this subject has been noticed, in the nave at Norwich (160); here Christ seems to have been first tied to the cross with ropes, but a soldier in armour is hammering a nail through one of his hands.

THE CRUCIFIXION is of course very frequent. Five fourteenth-century examples occur in Exeter Cathedral, one of them dating from the very first years of the century (97). Another of about the middle of the century shows Christ with a beard and makes him look like a very old man. At Nantwich is a Crucifixion which is very like the later Exeter ones. In the porch of Plympton St Mary, Devon, there is an extraordinarily crude example. There is also a rather crude example from the Lady Chapel at Ely (90), and another in the quire at Peterborough. The Crucifixion of early fourteenth-century date at Tewkesbury (214) is curious because the Cross itself is not carved. All the above have Our Lady and St John standing on either side of the Cross. At Salle the Cross is surrounded by various figures, and on one side Our Lady is fainting and is being supported by St John. In the nave at Norwich (161) many figures surround the Cross, but Our Lady and St John are not shown.

THE HARROWING OF HELL is found at Norwich in the cloisters, c. 1310, and in the nave, c. 1470 (162); the two representations have a general resemblance to each other, though separated in time by about 160 years; it is very probable that both were copied from illuminated manuscripts. In both, hell is

represented as a beast's mouth, wide open, with many teeth; Christ stands outside the mouth holding the Cross of the Resurrection with the vexillum in his
right hand, while with the left he is taking the hand of Adam to lead him out of
hell; the stigmata are shown in both bosses. In the earlier example five figures
are shown standing in hell's mouth, in the later eight.

THE RESURRECTION is one of the scenes in the series of bosses in the nave
at Tewkesbury (215) giving scenes from the life of Christ. Our Lord, holding the
Cross of the Resurrection with the vexillum, steps out of the tomb below which
are three Roman soldiers, and on either side there is a censing angel. There is
another example at Tewkesbury, in one of the apsidal chapels (221), where an
angel playing a musical instrument stands on either side of the risen Christ.
At Salle (193) and Norwich nave there are soldiers but no angels; at St Mary,
Redcliffe, there are kneeling angels but no soldiers; in the east walk of the
cloisters at Norwich there are angels and soldiers, the latter being depicted on
a very small scale; Nantwich also shows soldiers and angels. In the quire of
Peterborough the risen Christ is the only figure shown, and it is a very crude one.
Scenes connected with the Resurrection are found at Norwich both in the
cloisters and in the nave. In the north walk of the cloisters we find the women
at the empty tomb with an angel at the side, and soldiers round it; Christ
appearing to Mary Magdalene in the garden, the 'Noli me tangere'; Christ
appearing to the two disciples and the supper at Emmaus; Christ appearing to
the apostles; the incredulity of St Thomas. In the nave at Norwich we find
Christ appearing to St Peter who has a net over his garments; the 'Noli me
tangere'; and Christ appearing to the two disciples. The only other example of
the 'Noli me tangere' that I have noticed is in the north transept at Worcester
where it occurs by itself without any other scenes from the Resurrection.

THE ASCENSION is generally represented by a group of apostles with Our
Lady, and the feet of Our Lord and the hem of his garment are shown above,
disappearing into a cloud. The best example is in the nave at Tewkesbury where
twelve apostles and Our Lady are represented and the figures are standing; at
Salle, Our Lady and the apostles are kneeling and gazing upward; in the Lady
Chapel at Ely only six apostles and Our Lady are represented and St Peter and
St Andrew have nets over their clothes; in the nave at Norwich (163) eleven
apostles and Our Lady are standing round a mount, little more than their heads

being visible; the stigmata on Our Lord's feet are very clearly shown. In St Helen, Norwich (167), Our Lady and twelve apostles are indicated; over the apostles and round Our Lord's feet are fan-shaped objects, meant perhaps for rays of light. On the quire screen at York the disappearance into the cloud is represented in the usual way, but Our Lady and eleven apostles are kneeling and are all looking downwards and away from the ascending Christ. In the nave at York was a very curious Ascension; in the middle the soles of Christ's feet were represented in an oval; in compartments round were the heads of six figures with outspread hands; one of them was a woman; outside this again are shown the heads and hands of six more figures; no doubt these figures were meant for Our Lady and eleven apostles; the boss, which is described and figured by Browne,[1] has been reproduced in the modern roof.

CHRIST IN GLORY. This subject is of very frequent occurrence and is often found at the east end of a church, as for instance in the Lady Chapels of Winchester and Wells. At the east end of the Tewkesbury series Our Lord is shown seated, bare-headed and with both hands raised; between his feet is the globe; he is fully robed and his cloak is fastened by a large clasp at the neck. The example at Wells shows Our Lord seated on a bench with hands raised, in a cloak which, though fastened by a clasp, is open below to the waist showing the wound in the side; the stigmata are visible too on hands and feet; the figure is contained within a cusped border which is supported by four angels. Our Lord wears the Crown of Thorns. The Winchester (255) figure shows Our Lord with very long, flowing locks; he is fully robed, has the globe under his hand and resting on one knee, while his feet are on clouds. Around him are winged figures clothed in feathers, denoting one of the higher orders of angels. At Exeter there is another figure not surrounded by angels. In the south porch at Gloucester the central boss has a demi-figure of Christ, with both hands raised and stigmata on hands and side; around this boss are other bosses each bearing an angel, and the whole composition is evidently intended for Christ coming in glory.

THE LAST JUDGEMENT. This subject cannot always be differentiated from the last in art, and indeed one is only the continuation of the other. At Lichfield (117) Our Lord, as usual, has both hands raised, a cloak is fastened by

[1] John Browne, *The History of the Metropolitan Church of St Peter, York*, vol. II, Pl. CXVI.

a clasp at the neck, but is so draped as to leave the upper part of the body bare; doubtless the stigmata were once visible, but they are not now. Below Christ's feet are clouds and below these the globe. The only way that this representation differs from those of Christ in Glory is in the fact that there are two angels blowing large trumpets. In the Norwich (164) series, besides the angels blowing trumpets, an emperor and a pope are rising from the tomb, naked save for a crown and a tiara respectively.

THE IMAGE OF PITY was a very favourite subject in the later Middle Ages. Our Lord is shown as risen, but with the marks of the Passion on his hands, feet, and side, and usually with the Crown of Thorns on his head. Often he is shown standing in the open tomb, but the subject can be distinguished from the Resurrection as, in the Image of Pity, Our Lord does not carry the Cross with the vexillum. The subject is closely connected with the legend of the Mass of St Gregory. Large indulgences were granted to those who said certain prayers before such representations, which accounts for their frequent inclusion in books of hours from the late fourteenth century onwards, and they are found also in printed books of hours of the early part of the sixteenth century. On roof bosses this subject is rare, as might perhaps be expected, for the faithful could hardly say prayers before a roof boss. The only example I have come across is at Banwell where Our Lord stands in the tomb, the body, visible from the hips upward, being naked except for a loin cloth; he wears the Crown of Thorns, but the stigmata are not shown or are not now visible; the Cross, the spear and the sponge on the reed are depicted at the sides. In the Trinity in the west porch at Peterborough Christ is represented as the Image of Pity (180).

PASSION EMBLEMS. In paintings in books of hours the instruments and emblems of the Passion are often depicted in the background. In sculpture they are often shown carried by angels. In roof bosses some of the earliest examples are in the nave at Tewkesbury, where the Cross, the spear, the Crown of Thorns, and scourges are carried by angels; these date from the first half of the fourteenth century. Slightly later are the angels in the quire at Gloucester (105, 106) bearing the spear, the Crown of Thorns, the Cross, and the nails. At Lechlade angels carry the pillar, scourges, the Crown of Thorns, the coat and dice, the sponge on a spear, pincers, a lantern, and a label which may be meant for the label on the Cross; one angel also carries the Cross and one nail, another holds the other two nails. In the north porch at Salle is a figure of Christ surrounded by angels amongst whom are Passion emblems, including the Cross, spear, sponge on reed, pillar and cords, ladder and hammer.

In some of the wagon roofs in the West country we find isolated examples of Passion emblems either carried by angels, as the Crown of Thorns at Queen Camel, or by themselves as the Crown of Thorns at Newton St Cyres.

But by far the greater number of Passion emblems on roof bosses appear on shields, and by the end of the fifteenth century they were definitely used as the armorial bearings of Christ. In the library of the College of Arms there is a manuscript[1] which gives many of the usual emblems making them part of 'Arma Domini Nostri Jesu Christi'. Shields bearing the emblems are found on roof bosses all over the country. An early example is on the roof of the nave of St Cross, Winchester; it is associated with the arms of Wykeham and Beaufort, and the design on the boss is almost exactly the same as that on a shield on the brass of John de Camden in the chancel, the date of which is 1382. Here a number of Passion emblems are crowded onto one shield; the Cross with the Crown of Thorns looped over the head; the spear and the reed with the sponge arranged in saltire; two scourges and three nails on one side, and a hammer and the pillar of the flagellation on the other.

Later examples are so numerous that it is not possible to record them here. But they are found all over the country and especially on the wooden bosses on the wagon roofs of the West country.

But the greatest series of armorial Passion emblems is in the quire at Winchester (239-46). This magnificent series of wooden bosses of very early sixteenth-century date consists of armorial shields of Bishop Fox at the west end, Royal arms and badges in the centre, and the Passion emblems at the east end. Here we find the chalice of the Agony in the Garden, the Cross, the heart, hands, and feet emblems of the five wounds, Veronica's handkerchief, the pillar of the flagellation, the three nails, the spear, sponge and loin cloth, the money-bag of Judas and the thirty pieces of silver, Malchus with his ear severed by a sword, a smiting hand, a spitting Jew, the hammer and pincers, the ladder, the ewer and basin, a lantern, a torch and brazier, clubs, scourges, Our Lord's garment, the dice wherewith the soldiers cast lots, Judas kissing Christ, Pilate and his wife, the high priest, the cock, a pestle and mortar, the three pots of

[1] M. 5, f. 1. See also *Archaeologia*, vol. LXXVI, p. 165 and Plate XXVII.

ointment, and a hand holding hair. This emblem occurs occasionally; it might have been supposed to be the hair of St Mary Magdalene wherewith she wiped Our Lord's feet, but, as was pointed out to me by Professor Berliner, the hand is sometimes shown in a gauntlet which would indicate the hand as belonging to one of the soldiers present at the mocking. Dr M. R. James suggested that the emblem referred to the passage from Isaiah (l. 6): 'I gave my back to the smiters, and my cheeks to them that plucked off the hair.'

At St Just-in-Roseland (113, 114) in Cornwall there are flat painted bosses with Passion emblems painted on them; this is the only example I have come across of flat painted bosses; the paintwork is in a very decayed condition, but the designs are probably medieval, though they may have been touched up at a later date.

The Agnus Dei. This device is not nearly as common in England as it is in France. It is rather more common in the north of England and in Scotland where French influence was strong at times. At the eastern crossing at Canterbury (60) the central boss consists of the Lamb supporting with one foot the Cross and banner of the Resurrection, while round its head is the cross-bearing nimbus; the whole is supported by four angels. This boss was erected in 1178 and is certainly the work of the craftsmen who worked under William de Sens; the whole design is typically French, though it is doubtful whether anything so fine occurs in France. At Crondall (70) in Hampshire there is a somewhat similar boss, though without the angels; it must be of about the same date as the boss at Canterbury, and may possibly be the work of the same craftsmen. Another early example is in the quire at Durham (81), and this boss too is French in design, the lamb being carved in low relief on a nearly flat surface. There is one in the south aisle of the nave at Lincoln, and two in the chapter-house of York, one of which, however, is modern. There is one in the north porch at Exeter, one in Pluscardine Abbey, and two rather late ones in the crypt of Glasgow Cathedral. Late wooden examples are found at Ripon; Selworthy, Somerset; Mattingley, Hants; St Andrew Undershaft in London, and St Peter Mancroft, Norwich.

In the Divinity School at Oxford there is an Agnus Dei which shows the Lamb couchant on a book; the Lamb is almost always represented standing, though there is another couchant example among the painted bosses at St Just-in-Roseland.

And here we may consider the representations of Pentecost. I know of only four, one of which, that in the nave at York, is modern, but it is copied from an engraving of the original boss which was destroyed by fire in 1829.[1]

By far the best representation of Pentecost is at Tewkesbury (216) where Our Lady and the twelve apostles are standing together with the Dove flying down from above; it is an extremely good carving. The example from the nave at Norwich is not nearly so good; here Our Lady and six apostles, one, St John, beardless, seem to be seated, while above them is the Dove, not very well carved, with rays of light descending between the figures. In the fourth bay of the north walk of the cloisters at Norwich, Our Lady is seated surrounded by the twelve apostles, and above is the Dove; the boss is much mutilated and several heads are missing, including that of Our Lady. The York example was very peculiar; in the centre the Dove was represented upside down, for its feet appear tucked up under its body; this is surrounded by a circle, outside which are the heads and raised hands of Our Lady and five apostles, one, St John, beardless; another circle surrounds these and outside it are the heads and shoulders of six bearded apostles, with their hands holding on to the outer circle. Ribbon-like objects come from the beak of the Dove and end in the mouths or under the beards of the surrounding figures.

[1] John Browne, *History of the Metropolitan Church of St Peter*, York, Plate cxviii.

CHAPTER III

THE LIFE OF OUR LADY; SAINTS; ANGELS

The Life of Our Lady

INCIDENTS of the life of Our Lady occur, as might be supposed, on a great number of bosses. Some of these, such as those connected with the Last Supper, the Crucifixion, the Ascension, Pentecost, and others, have been dealt with in Chapter II.

It may perhaps be interesting to record the number of cases in which scenes connected with Our Lady are represented on roof bosses:

St Anne and the Virgin	2
Annunciation	21
Visitation	7
Nativity	7
Magi and Shepherds at Bethlehem	10
Presentation	4
Circumcision	4
Virgin and Child	16
Assumption	13
Coronation	32

There are no doubt other examples that are unknown to me, but these numbers are probably an indication of the relative numbers in which these scenes occur.

St Anne and the Virgin are found at Ottery St Mary (170) and Nantwich; in both cases the figures are standing and St Anne holds a book out of which she is teaching the Virgin. The Visitation is found in the nave at Lichfield, in the Lady Chapel at Ely, and once in the nave, three times in the transepts, and once in the cloisters at Norwich.

The Annunciation occurs in many places and in all periods of Gothic sculpture. One of the earliest is in the west aisle of the north transept of Westminster Abbey (226); it is very badly weathered, but it has been an extremely graceful figure; Our Lady is seated on a chair with her left hand on a book on a book-rest; of Gabriel only half the figure is represented; between them is the lily pot; Gabriel has a scroll on which there are still traces of lettering; on the right there seem to have been the figures of two other angels. In the south walk of the cloisters at Norwich is an extremely good carving; both figures are standing, Gabriel with his hand raised in benediction; his wings are extended. In the Lichfield example (119) in the south aisle of the quire a large Dove has its beak close to Our Lady's ear. At Ottery St Mary (171) Gabriel is on the right-hand side, which is unusual, and there is no lily pot. On the beautiful little pendent boss at Patrington, Our Lady is kneeling with both hands extended; of Gabriel only the upper part is visible, the rest seems to be hidden by the lily. In the Lady Chapel at Ely only demi figures are shown; Gabriel's wings are hardly indicated; he holds a scroll with the lettering AVA GRATIA P. At Ripon both figures are standing, and one of Gabriel's wings passes behind Our Lady's head; the lily pot is very prominent. On one of the small bosses on the quire screen at York, Our Lady, curiously, is turning away from Gabriel. At Nantwich, Gabriel is kneeling before Our Lady and the book-rest is between them; she has her right hand on the book, and she and Gabriel are clasping what seems to be the stem of the lily. In the north aisle of the nave at Worcester, and in the east aisle of the south transept at St Mary, Redcliffe, each figure stands under a crocketed arch. In the late fifteenth-century example in the nave at Norwich (158) Gabriel is kneeling on one knee; he has four wings and has an ermine tippet; his label shows signs of lettering. In the very late and rather crude example at St Andrew, Worcester, the head of an old man, no doubt God the Father, is seen just above the three-headed lily. In the late boss in the porch of St John the Baptist, Peterborough, Our Lady is shown with her outer cloak thrown back; it is fastened at the breast with a large clasp; her undergown fits very close at the waist and is laced down the front. In the rather crude representation in the quire at Peterborough the lily and lily pot take up quite half of the composition; Gabriel, with a scroll, is on the right-hand side.

The representations of the Virgin and Child are perhaps more suitably described here than under the heading of the life of Christ. One of the earliest examples is in the Lady Chapel at Worcester (284) where Our Lady is seated with the Child on her knee; she is crowned and holds what looks like a lily stem with fruit on the end; but the bosses in the east end of the Cathedral have suffered so much restoration that little reliance can be placed on them as medieval sculptures. There is another much later example in the cloisters which has been taken for the same subject, but the middle part of the boss has apparently been renewed and it seems to me doubtful whether it was originally meant for a Virgin and Child. A mid-thirteenth-century example in the muniment room at Westminster Abbey is unfortunately much mutilated; there were angels, possibly censing on each side. In the late thirteenth-century Lady Chapel at Chester (72) is an extremely good example, with kneeling censing angels on each side, and in the nearly contemporaneous chapter-house at Christ Church, Oxford, there is also an excellent Virgin and Child, where the Virgin is handing a fruit to the Child. In the fourteenth-century chapel of St John the Baptist at Exeter the Virgin is standing and holds a fruit in her right hand. Of nearly the same date are the two examples at Ottery St Mary (172); in one the Virgin, seated, is handing a pear to the Child, in the other she is standing and the Child holds a fruit. At Abbey Dore an ecclesiastic is kneeling before the Virgin and Child. A wooden carving of early date in the cloisters at Lincoln is very badly mutilated, but it has been a very delicate carving. In the Lady Chapel at Ely (89) only the head and shoulders of the Virgin and only the head of the Child are seen through surrounding foliage.

Other examples from the nave and south transept of St Mary, Redcliffe, and from Selworthy and Plympton call for no special comment.

No very early example of the Assumption has been noted. In the Lady Chapel at Ely (91) Our Lady stands in a vesica piscis supported on either side by a monk and by a woman crowned and in a nun's habit, no doubt St Etheldreda; there are also two angel supporters. At Lichfield (120) Our Lady stands under a cusped arch with several angels supporting it. Under the quire screen at York at the entrance to the quire Our Lady is surrounded by rays of light; outside these is an oval of conventional foliage which is supported by two angels and two archangels; the boss has been painted in modern times and may have suffered some restoration. In the very small boss in the chapel of Our Lady of the Pew at Westminster (232) six angels support Our Lady and the figures are surrounded by conventional clouds. At Nantwich Our Lady stands in a cusped vesica piscis supported by four angels. In the Audley Chapel at Hereford Our Lady stands surrounded by a circular plate over which rays of light radiate; her hair is hanging over her shoulders to well below the waist; she is crowned. In the quire at Norwich is a somewhat similar figure, though not nearly so artistically rendered; there is a wreath of roses outside the rays; here too the Virgin is crowned. A much better Assumption is in the Bauchon Chapel, where

Our Lady wearing a triple tiara is surrounded by rays of light radiating from her; four or more angels support her by taking hold of some of the rays. Crowned figures surrounded by rays occur also in the porch of Walpole St Peter, and in the quire at Peterborough, the latter are demi-figures. There is a very fine boss in the Lady Chapel at Winchester (256) where Our Lady, crowned, stands within a cusped circle and is supported by six angels; she wears an ermine cloak.

It will be noticed that several of these Assumptions show the Virgin crowned; this of course is incorrect, as the Assumption should precede the Coronation in the iconography.

There is a very interesting Assumption in the west porch at Peterborough (181); Our Lady, not crowned, is supported by four angels and she carries a large belt with a strap-fastening; this is an allusion to the legend that St Thomas was not present at the Assumption and 'would not believe this. And anon the girdle with which her body was girt came to him from the air, which he received, and thereby he understood that she was assumpt into heaven.'[1]

There is an Assumption in the porch of Cley-next-the-Sea, but it is very badly worn.

The Coronation of the Virgin is represented on roof bosses in several different ways.

1. The figures of Christ and the Virgin are seated, and Christ is placing the crown on Our Lady's head; Christ has either a book in, or a globe in or under, his left hand. The best example is in the presbytery at Ely (85); there is another good one in the quire at Exeter (98), where Christ is beardless; there is another in the same Cathedral in the north aisle of the nave. Others are at Abbey Dore, Bishopstone, Lichfield, north quire aisle, St Mary, Redcliffe, east aisle of south transept, and Worcester, north aisle of the nave. Among the early wooden bosses in the cloisters at Lincoln is a Coronation which is so damaged that it is not possible to say whether it belongs to this class or to the next.

2. Very similar to No. 1, but Our Lady is already crowned and Christ is blessing. There are three very fine examples: in the Angel quire at Lincoln (121) dating from about 1270, in the nave at Tewkesbury (217) about 1330, and at Ottery St Mary (173) probably of a slightly later date. Others are at Buckland Monachorum, Ely Lady Chapel, demi-figures, Gloucester (nave), Nantwich, Norwich, St Helen's Hospital, where twelve angels surround the other figures, Tewkesbury, St Margaret's Chapel, and York on the quire screen.

[1] *The Golden Legend* (Temple Classics), vol. IV, p. 241.

3. Christ and Our Lady are seated side by side and an angel is placing a crown on the Virgin's head. Probably the earliest example of a boss of the Coronation is of this type; it is at Westminster, in the bay that is common to the south aisle and the west aisle of the south transept; unfortunately it is badly mutilated, but there is little doubt about the subject; Christ is seated on the left-hand side which is unusual. There is a very charming Coronation of this type in the retroquire at Beverley Minster (48) at the back of the screen. Another example is in the quire at Lichfield, badly damaged, and clumsily repaired; and perhaps one of the best is in the north porch at Denton.

4. The Father and the Son are seated on a throne with the Virgin on a lower seat between them, while above is the Dove. There are two examples of this type in the cloisters at Norwich, one in the fifth bay of the north walk, the other in the twelfth bay of the west walk. The first has been a very beautiful composition, and even now, with the heads missing, it can be seen how good it was; the figure of Our Lady is extremely graceful and delicate. The second example is extremely elaborate; Our Lady is crowned with a triple crown, and around are many angels, two of a higher order; the boss is much damaged, but even in its original state it must have lacked the grace of the first example.

One of the small bosses on the quire screen at York is a Coronation of this type; the Virgin is standing, her feet hidden in clouds; the Father wears a triple crown and holds the globe, and the Son is placing a crown on Our Lady's head. The head of the Dove is missing and the crown has either been broken and clumsily repaired or it was never finished. In the Bauchon Chapel at Norwich the Father and the Son are both placing the crown on Our Lady's head, and the Dove is also holding in its beak a cross on the top of the tiara; its wings overshadow the other two figures of the Trinity; the Father wears a crown and the Son the Crown of Thorns. Under the tower of St Andrew, Worcester, is a Coronation of this type, but the Virgin is seated between the Father and the Son on the same level; the Dove above comes out of clouds; the Father wears a crown and the Son is probably meant to be wearing the Crown of Thorns. In the porch at Worsted is a very badly weathered example; the Dove had a cross-bearing nimbus.

5. The three Persons of the Trinity are represented as three old men, and the Virgin is in front of them. I have only come across two examples; one is the weathered but still very fine boss in the centre of the south walk of the cloisters at Worcester (288); the three Persons are all exactly similar as far as one can see;

they are bearded and bare-headed; Our Lady, seated in front of them, is wearing a triple tiara. The very badly mutilated boss in the Salisbury Chapel at Christ-church, Hampshire, is almost certainly a Coronation of this type. The Three Persons are seated and the Virgin is kneeling before them.[1]

There is a very badly worn Coronation in the porch at Wymondham, but I have no note as to which class it belongs.

There are other scenes in which Our Lady appears, the majority of them at Norwich, either in the scenes from the early life of Christ in the transepts, various scenes in the cloisters and in the Bauchon Chapel. Here too, it may be mentioned, is a very good Pieta, Our Lady supporting the dead body of Christ; it is a corbel, not a boss; I cannot recall any other example of this motif in medieval sculpture in this country.

And here mention may be made of the arms of Our Lady (296-9), for as Christ was assigned armorial bearings in late medieval times (see Chapter II, p. 37) so was Our Lady. In Bristol Cathedral they appear twice, once as two swords piercing a heart, in reference to Luke ii. 35: 'Yea, a sword shall pierce through thy own soul also.' On another boss the heart is pierced by one sword and there are wings on each side of the heart, in allusion, doubtless, to the wings of the Archangel of the Annunciation. In St Mary, Redcliffe, are two rather similar bosses, and there is another in St Mary, Beverley. In the south transept at Hereford, and in the cloisters at Canterbury there is a heart flanked with wings, probably intended for the arms of Our Lady.

Saints

A large number of saints are depicted on roof bosses. The apostles occur of course in the various scenes from the Life of Christ, such as the Tewkesbury series, the New Testament scenes in the western half of the nave, the scenes from the early Life of Christ in the transepts, and in various scenes from the Gospel story in the cloisters at Norwich. All twelve apostles appear in St Helen, Norwich, and in St Andrew, Worcester, and a number of them in the nave at Selworthy.

The four evangelists are found on the remarkable border to the well-hole over the Chapel of the Nine Altars at Durham, where each has his emblem beside him. They are also in the cloisters at Norwich; unfortunately all their heads

[1] Described in the *V.C.H. Hampshire*, vol. v, p. 103 as the Countess of Salisbury kneeling before the Trinity, but in my opinion it is a Coronation.

were knocked off, though they have been replaced by modern restorations. The emblems of the evangelists are found in a great number of places.

Besides these a number of individual saints are to be found. St Anne teaching the Virgin is at Ottery St Mary (170) and at Nantwich. At Exeter is the Crucifixion of St Andrew who is being tied to the cross with cords. St Barbara is found as a demi-figure in the deanery at Carlisle. St Christopher appears, as far as my records go, only at Selworthy and in the Norwich cloisters; his absence from roof bosses is remarkable considering how often he appears on wall paintings. St Edmund, being shot with arrows, is on a small boss in the chapel dedicated to him at Tewkesbury (220). Edward the Confessor is in St Helen, Norwich, and his vision of Our Lord while at mass is depicted in the cloisters at Norwich (144).

In the north aisle of Ugborough Church is a curious figure of a blacksmith forging a horse-shoe, which has been taken to be a representation of St Eligius or Eloi.

In Ely Cathedral there are, as one would expect, several representations of St Etheldreda. The finest is the one in Bishop Northwold's presbytery (86), over the spot where her shrine stood. In the Lady Chapel there is an Assumption (91) flanked on either side by a monk and by St Etheldreda, and at the west end of the same chapel is a rather confused mass of figures representing the translation of the saint (92) in which the stone coffin mentioned by Bede is quite clearly shown. At Christ Church, Oxford, there are three figures of St Frideswide, two late ones in the quire and one quite early one in the chapter-house. One would expect St George with the Dragon to appear on a large number of bosses, but I have found him in only six churches. At Banwell in Somerset there are a large number of bosses of the saint on horseback slaying the dragon. The other examples are in the cloisters at Norwich, at Wootton Courtenay, at Worcester where he is shown in the cloisters of the Cathedral and under the tower at the church of St Andrew.

St John in the cauldron of oil is found in the crypt of St Mary in the Palace of Westminster, and in the cloisters at Norwich; here too is found the legend of St John and the poisoned cup, and the representation of his assumption with the grave filled with manna, and above it St John as an old man borne upwards by angels.

St John the Baptist is found over and over again in the transepts at Norwich. Here we find Zacharias coming from the Temple, dumb and writing the name of John; we find the birth of John the Baptist and his circumcision; John teaching in the wilderness, baptizing in the Jordon, and then baptizing Christ. Then we see him rebuking Herod, sent to prison, beheaded, his head brought into Herod's feast and finally his burial. He is baptizing Christ in the nave at Norwich, and appears also in the scene of Herod's feast in the cloisters (142). In other places he appears in his camel-hair garment and holding the lamb, as at Patrington, Ottery St Mary, and Exeter.

St John of Beverley is seen side by side with Athelstan both in the chancel (19) and in the nave of St Mary, Beverley.

St Joseph is only found in scenes of the Nativity or early childhood of Christ. When he is found by himself on any bosses in the transepts at Norwich it is in connection with neighbouring bosses dealing with the Nativity. He is shown taking to him Mary his wife, asking her pardon for his doubting, going with her to Bethlehem, an angel speaking to him, the flight into Egypt, and seeking the Child Jesus.

St Katherine, easily recognized by her broken wheel, is to be found at Patrington, Selworthy, Widecombe-in-the-Moor, at Norwich in the cloisters, and at St Helen, and on a very elaborate boss in the crypt of St Mary in the Palace of Westminster. In the same crypt is the martyrdom of St Laurence, who despite his high place in the hagiarchy only appears here and in the Norwich cloisters as far as I have been able to ascertain. In the crypt at Westminster too is St Margaret slaying the Dragon.

Another saint with a very popular appeal is St Martin, but he like St George is only found twice, once in the south-west tower at Lincoln, where, riding on a stallion, he divides his cloak for a beggar who lies prone almost under his horse's hoofs; he is found again in the cloisters at Norwich.

St Mary Magdalene appears in the Supper at Bethany, coming to the tomb with a pot of ointment, and in the 'Noli me tangere' scene, both in the nave and in the cloisters at Norwich; the 'Noli me tangere' is also found at Nantwich and in the north transept at Worcester. St Michael, like St George, might be expected to occur more often than he does, considering how apt for carving on a roof boss is his fight with the dragon. As it is he is found in St Edmund's Chapel at Tewkesbury, in the nave at Sherborne (205), in the cloisters at Worcester, and at York in the south transept and twice on the quire screen. St Nicholas, another popular saint, is only found on two bosses in the cloisters at Norwich; they are not very clear, but they are attributed to St Nicholas by Dr M. R. James.

St Paul is to be found three times at Exeter (104) and once each at Plympton St Mary and Selworthy, all be it noted in the West country and not far from the sea. St Peter, besides being seen in the nave, transepts, and cloisters at Norwich in various New Testament scenes, is also at Plympton St Mary and Selworthy. A saint being crucified head downwards in the Norwich cloisters is attributed to St Peter by Dr M. R. James, but the figure has no beard and St Peter without a beard seems rather improbable. The Stoning of St Stephen occurs both in the crypt of St Mary and in St Stephen's cloisters of the Palace of Westminster. His martyrdom also occurs in the cloisters at Norwich. St Thomas the Apostle is in the nave and the cloisters at Norwich, both examples showing him putting his hand into Our Lord's side.

St Thomas of Canterbury appears in three cathedrals; the earliest is in the Lady Chapel at Chester dating from the latter part of the thirteenth century. At Exeter there is a very fine example dating from about 1350 (Frontispiece); it is one of the three or four outstanding roof bosses in the country; the whole scene of the murder is depicted on the small space of the boss; the kneeling saint, the four knights, FitzUrse, with a bear on his shield, striking the first blow; at the side stands Grimm, the cross-bearer, and close beside is the altar with two cruets on a small shelf. Two examples are to be found in the Norwich cloisters, but they are much mutilated; close beside these are the monks finding Becket's body, the translation, and Henry II being scourged by the monks at the shrine (143).

St Werburgh is on a boss in the Abbey gate at Chester.

There are a number of saints that I have not mentioned above which have been identified in the cloisters at Norwich by Dr M. R. James.[1] They include SS. Basil, Clement, Dennis, Eustace, Giles, James-the-Greater, James-the-Less, Lucy, Theophilus.

Angels

Angels occur with great frequency on roof bosses. The earliest representation is on the Agnus Dei boss in the centre of the eastern crossing at Canterbury (60); round the boss, in the angles made by the vaulting-ribs, are four angels; the date of this boss is 1178. Angle figures of angels are fairly common on roof bosses in France, but this is the only important example I know of in this country. There is, however, a small example in the north aisle of the quire in

[1] M. R. James, *The Sculptured Bosses in the Cloisters of Norwich Cathedral*. Norwich and Norfolk Archaeological Society.

Westminster Abbey, where there are four angels, one in each angle, but there is no central carving. Most of the early representations of angels, or perhaps one should rather say archangels, are in carvings of the Annunciation; a thirteenth-century example, unfortunately much weathered, is in the west aisle of the north transept in Westminster Abbey (226), and other examples of later date occur in Annunciation bosses. Angels are also found in other representations, as at Norwich in the Apocalypse scenes in the cloisters, fourteenth century, the Old and New Testament scenes in the nave, late fifteenth century, and in the scenes from the early life of Christ in the transepts, early sixteenth century.

Angels are usually represented on roof bosses holding some object in their hands. In the fourteenth century and later these are sometimes Passion emblems not on shields.

Considerably commoner are angels carrying shields on which Passion emblems are displayed heraldically as the armorial bearings of Christ; these became very common in the fifteenth century; there are perhaps more of them on corbels than on actual bosses. In the same way shields of arms, sometimes royal, sometimes of a diocese, sometimes of some family, are borne by angels, and these too became very common in the fifteenth century, so that examples can be seen in numberless churches. A very good one is to be found on the vaulting under the tower at Tewkesbury. In the quire at Chichester the arms of St Richard are carried by an angel, in the south aisle of the nave at Winchester the royal arms are so carried, and in the same bay the arms of Wykeham are carried by no less than three angels. In St Stephen's cloister, Westminster, was an angel holding a shield on which Wolsey's cardinal's hat was depicted as though it were an armorial bearing, while another held a shield on which a pomegranate appears as a charge. At Blythburgh (69) there are wooden bosses on the rafters bearing the conventional representation of clouds, and on each side of them, east and west as though rising from the clouds, are extremely fine figures of angels carrying shields of arms; they have very long, outstretched wings that have every appearance of being original.

Censing angels are found occasionally; there are several in the nave at Tewkesbury, and at Worcester there are two angels censing an archbishop in the south transept (285), and two censing a bishop in the nave; in the cloisters there are angels swinging their censers towards the boss of the Coronation of the Virgin. In the choir of angels at Westminster there is an angel carrying a censer and an incense boat.

Angels playing on musical instruments are found fairly often from quite early times to the end of the Gothic period. Several are to be found in the choir of angels in Westminster Abbey (222-5). In the nave at Tewkesbury are a number dating from the first half of the fourteenth century, and in the quire at Gloucester (107-12) of a slightly later date. Another much later set is at Buckland Monachorum in Devon, these being wooden bosses. There are many examples where a few angels are found playing instruments, as in the south aisle of the nave at Winchester (260), on the small bosses on the quire screen at York, and in the chapel of St Edmund at Tewkesbury, where three angels surround the risen Christ (221), one playing a viol, one a trumpet, and one some other instrument which is not very clearly shown. Very many more instances might be cited. In the north transept at Norwich the souls of the Innocents are being led to heaven by angels, one of whom is playing a lute.

A few angels are found carrying books, one occurs on a wooden boss at the west end of the nave at Worsted,[1] a very well executed little figure; at Wootton Courtenay another equally well carved figure of an angel seated also holds a book.

Many other objects are found carried by angels; crowns at Burwell, Furneaux Pelham, and on the quire screen at York; a church at the east end of the quire at Christchurch, Hampshire; a castle in St Stephen's cloisters, Westminster (twice); a mitre in the sacristy at Selby; a portcullis at Winchester and Windsor; a rose at Chester, Wells and Windsor; the sun and the moon at St Mary, Bury St Edmunds, and a sundial in the choir of angels at Westminster.

Angels by themselves, carrying no object, are also found occasionally. There is a very well carved figure in the midst of foliage in St Hugh's quire at Lincoln, though the style and carving show that it dates from the time of the Angel quire. Of a much later date are the small wooden figures of angels at Cawston in Norfolk; some of these have lost their wings, but figures of angels can be recognized, as they are nearly always shown wearing an alb and amice. A very good late example is the early sixteenth-century demi-figure in the south aisle of the quire at Winchester; the angel is looking upward with hands upraised; it is a particularly pleasing composition.

In many cases where wings have been destroyed during periods of iconoclasm, or have been lost through decay they have been replaced in the nineteenth

[1] A book is often the emblem of the Cherubim, but in this case it is plain that the figure is an ordinary angel; see Philip B. Chatwin, F.S.A., 'The Decoration of the Beauchamp Chapel, Warwick, with special reference to the Sculptures', *Archaeologia*, vol. 77, p. 322.

century, and occasionally wings have been given to figures which had not been meant for angels, as on a boss in the quire at Ripon; a photograph of this boss, taken many years ago when the bosses were taken down during restorations, shows a crowned figure with no signs that it had ever had wings.

Angels of the higher orders seldom appear on roof bosses except Gabriel on bosses connected with the Annunciation, and Michael slaying the Dragon.

Archangels can be recognized because they are represented with feathered bodies and legs, and they are not habited in an alb like an angel. There is an archangel kneeling in the Creation bosses at the east end of the nave at Norwich, and there are two more, also kneeling, by the boss representing the Ascension; and Gabriel appears in the Annunciation (158) boss in the same series; he is shown with two pair of wings, and with a feathered body unclothed except for an ermine tippet. In the chancel of St Mary, Beverley, is a demi-figure of an archangel holding a crown, and himself crowned; in the Lady Chapel there are three three-quarter length figures of archangels, all feathered and unclothed except for ermine tippets; one holds Veronica's handkerchief, another a heart.

In the south aisle of the nave of St Mary, Bury St Edmunds, is a three-quarter length winged figure crowned and wearing, apparently, a stole, but otherwise unclothed, and with a feathered body; in each hand he holds a large chalice with the host in each; the figure issues from conventional clouds. In the nave at Cawston there are three bosses with archangels, all small figures; two are demi-figures, one has a feathered body, the other has no feathers, but the absence of an alb differentiates it from the figure of an ordinary angel. The third figure is represented standing with wings extended; he has feathered upper arms, wears a tippet and perhaps another garment; but the figure is immediately placed in the higher order of angels by having two pairs of wings.

Archangels surround Christ in Glory on the boss in the Lady Chapel at Winchester (255).

CHAPTER IV

MEN AND WOMEN

BESIDES figures of saints there are many men and women depicted on bosses, and many more men than women.

Perhaps two of the most interesting are in the nave at Exeter, one representing a bishop and one a kneeling ecclesiastic. There can be no doubt that the bishop is intended for Grandison (103), and it has all the appearance of being meant for a portrait and not just a conventional bishop; Grandison is found in the latter guise at Ottery St Mary, and a comparison of the two bosses strongly suggests that the first is a portrait. Grandison's boss is just to the east of the boss with the representation of the murder of St Thomas of Canterbury. Just to the west of the latter is the representation of an ecclesiastic holding a scroll on which the words 'Ora pro me sc Tome' can just be made out. There can be little doubt that this figure is meant for Canon William de Weston who was Grandison's right-hand man. This figure too has the appearance of being a portrait and not just a conventional figure; the canon wears an almuce with a hood turned back, leaving the head bare. This boss has been described[1] as representing St Dunstan, the label being described as 'really the curved frame of a large harp, the back of which is clearly visible resting against the left shoulder of the figure. This undoubtedly marks the "priest" as St Dunstan.' A long-focus lens, however, shows unmistakably that there is lettering and that the object in question is certainly a label.

Two other figures of kneeling ecclesiastics have been noted (50, 51), one at Blunham, the other at Great St Mary at Cambridge, where an ecclesiastic is kneeling before a crucifix; this figure was supposed to be a king, possibly Henry VII, but here again a long-focus lens reveals the true explanation.

There are not many bosses with full-length figures of ecclesiastics, with the exception of saints and bishops, but in the cloisters at Norwich priests appear in some of the scenes; in the vision of Edward the Confessor a priest is represented saying mass (144). On another boss is an altar on which stand a chalice, covered by a corporal, and an open missal; in front of the altar a priest is

[1] E. K. Prideaux and G. R. Holt Shafto, *Bosses and Corbels of Exeter Cathedral*, p. 175.

administering the Eucharist to three boys; the subject is the legend of the Jew of Bourges which tells how a Jewish boy, with two companions, received the sacrament; the boy's father put him into a heated oven from which he was delivered by Our Lady. On the left of the boss the boy can be seen being pushed into the oven by his father.

In the west aisle of the south transept of St Mary, Redcliffe, is a priest hearing a man's confession; the priest is seated and has his right hand raised as though giving absolution; the penitent is kneeling with his hands together in an attitude of prayer; it is notable that he wears a skull-cap.

There is a full-length figure of a pope under the tower of St Andrew, Worcester; part of the tiara is broken off, but enough remains to show that it was intended for the triple crown; two small figures, a man and a woman, kneel before him, possibly they may represent the donors of the roof; the pope may also be a saint, for rays of light shine from behind him. This is the only full-length figure of a pope that has been noted. There are, however, four heads of popes which will be noticed later.[1]

There are two archbishops in the south transept at Worcester, one with censing angels, probably St Dunstan (285), and there is one in the quire at Christ Church, Oxford. Worcester has also two bishops in the Lady Chapel, one in the nave, with censing angels, and several in the cloisters; here on one boss there are two bishops with the Virgin and Child between them. In the south walk of the cloisters there is the recumbent figure of a bishop with a tree growing out of him after the manner of the Tree of Jesse (289) (see Appendix under Worcester). Ripon has three bosses with bishops, one of them being seated beside a king. In the quire of Christ Church, Oxford, is a bishop with two attendants. At Selby there is a demi-figure in a mitre with an open book and a bird on each side of him. It is possible that some or all of these archbishops and bishops may be intended for saints.

Of kings perhaps the most curious are two in the north transept of Bristol Cathedral; one is completely naked except for his crown, the other partially so; I have no hesitation in ascribing these to Edward II in his death agony; in one boss (29) the king is actually pointing with his finger to the exact spot where was inserted the red-hot iron that killed him.

In the cloisters at Worcester are a number of kings in the Jesse Tree series; one of them, holding a harp, must be meant for David (291). In the quire at

[1] See Chapter v.

Exeter is a king seated crossed-legged on an oak branch, and holding a sceptre; this may be meant for the King-of-the-May (see p. 67). In the north walk of the cloisters at Norwich is a spirited representation of a king attacking a lion with a dagger, ascribed by Dr M. R. James to Richard Cœur de Lion. On the quire screen at York is a king seated and holding a spear and a mace, and supported by an eagle and some other beast. Round the base of the lantern at Ely are several kings with the lower part of their bodies hidden by foliage. Coming to extremely late times is a demi-figure portrait boss of Charles I and his Queen on the vaulting under the tower at Winchester (268).

Apart from heads, there are a very few figures of queens; in the Angel quire at Lincoln there is a queen with two lap-dogs (122). At Overbury is a demi-figure of a queen, who may also perhaps be a saint. In the crypt of St Mary at Westminster is St Margaret slaying the Dragon. In St Helen at Norwich is a queen in a wimple, holding a distaff. At the base of the lantern at Ely there is certainly one queen, perhaps two, among the kings; like them, they too have the lower part of the body hidden by foliage.

Figures of ordinary men and women, apart from saints, kings, queens and bishops, are not found very early; perhaps among the earliest are the figures of the man and woman kissing across a vaulting-rib in the north aisle of the Angel quire at Lincoln (130). Making the vaulting-rib part of the picture is a device that is found in several places; at Exeter an old man and a young woman seem to have met by climbing across a vaulting-rib, and in the Norwich cloisters a youth is climbing up a rib, as though up a tree, and is looking back over his shoulder at an old man below who seems to be searching for him.

Among the early figures of women two of the best are in the wooden bosses in the cloisters at Lincoln; despite their decayed state they can still be seen to be very graceful figures.

In stained glass we sometimes find the donor of the window, and perhaps his wife also, represented kneeling. What are probably similar figures are found at Croscombe where there is a woman with a spindle lying in front of her, while opposite is the kneeling figure of a man with a pair of shears behind him; both figures have large scrolls over them, but nothing in the way of inscription is now visible (78, 79).

We find a number of figures of men on horseback. There are many at Norwich in the bosses dealing with the Apocalypse in the cloisters, and those dealing with the Magi in the transepts. St George has already been mentioned

(Chapter III). In the nave at Exeter there is a man in armour fighting a dragon; it is not typical of St George, and I do not feel that it is meant to represent him. The man is in chain-mail armour with a surcoat over it, and he wears a helmet with the visor closed; both the man and the horse wear a crest like a fan. There are two dragons, one biting the knight's waist, the other biting the horse's fore-leg; the presence of the two dragons is fairly conclusive evidence that the figure is not that of St George. There is a very much later, and a very much less artistic example of a man in armour with his horse trampling on a dragon in the nave of St Mary, Beverley. Besides the horsemen in the Apocalypse bosses in the cloisters at Norwich there is an amusing one in the south walk of a man falling from his horse which has obviously stumbled. In the north aisle of the nave at St Mary, Beverley, is a man seated well back on a horse and in front of him he has two large and well-filled saddle-bags, and in the Lady Chapel is another very similar figure. At Selby (198) there is a man riding on an ass, he has a cutlass in his right hand and with his left he is holding on to one of the ass's ears; there are no reins. In the south walk of the cloisters at Canterbury there are three shaggy men, one of whom is riding a horse and has just transfixed a boar with his spear.

There are a number of men fighting with a lion; some of these are no doubt meant for Samson; there are three examples at Exeter, one at Lichfield, and one in the nave at Norwich. Here too Samson appears with Delilah shearing his locks, and on another boss bound by Delilah, and on yet another he is carrying off the gates of Gaza (156).

A certain number of Old Testament figures are to be found besides Samson, but they are not very numerous except in the Old Testament series in the nave at Norwich. Here we get the creation of Adam and also that of Eve (146), the Fall (147), Lamech killing Cain (148), Noah building the Ark (149) and planting vines, and various scenes connected with the story of the Flood, including the Ark itself (150) and Noah's drunkenness; we find the histories of Abraham, Isaac, and Jacob, of Joseph and of Moses (151), including the drowning of the Egyptians in the Red Sea (152); we have David and Goliath, and David sitting crowned as king, and just before coming to the New Testament scenes we have Solomon, crowned and seated on a throne, with a sword in his left hand and a church in his right, as the builder of the Temple (157).

Abraham with the souls of the just in his bosom is found in the quire at Durham (82), an aged man seated and holding the two ends of a napkin within which are three small figures. In the muniment room at Westminster Abbey is a very much worn boss which seems to represent the same subject.

The Fall is depicted in several other places besides Norwich; in the Lady Chapel at Ely, the cloisters at Canterbury, the nave at St Mary, Beverley, the cloisters at Norwich, and in the north aisle of the nave of St Mary, Bury St Edmunds. At Ripon the Fall itself is not shown, but there is a representation of the Expulsion, and of God speaking to Eve before the Expulsion (Genesis iii. 16). In the south aisle of the nave at Winchester are Adam and Eve after the Expulsion, dressed in skins (259).

Besides the Norwich examples David is found at Westminster in the west aisle of the north transept, an early example, at Lincoln in a Jesse Tree (123), at Exeter, and in the cloisters at Worcester (291).

Prophets are found in the FitzAlan Chapel at Arundel (15), and prophets discoursing with apostles in the south aisle of the Angel quire at Lincoln (124), and another boss perhaps shows Nathan speaking to David (125).

Judas chewed by the Devil, as in Dante's *Inferno*, canto 34, is found in the south transept at Amesbury (292); the Devil has a huge open mouth; Judas, who is naked, has his head and shoulders within the Devil's mouth, most of his body being without, including his arms which are held by the Devil. In one of the bosses from the fifteenth-century nave at Southwark the same scene is depicted (293), but here only the lower part of the body and the legs are visible, the upper part being between the Devil's clenched teeth; Judas wears a short tunic. Another example of the same subject is reported from Wootton-under-Edge.

The Occupations of the Months, so often represented in medieval art, hardly appear at all on roof bosses. The only examples noted are in the wooden bosses in the cloisters at Lincoln;[1] here in the east walk there are four bosses which seem to belong to the series; all are much mutilated; on one a man is bending forward holding something with both hands; he may be meant to be cutting down a tree; a second looks like a man sowing; a third is evidently a man killing a pig, and a fourth is a man seated and holding a bowl, perhaps meant for feasting. The last two subjects are usually for December and January, but one occasionally finds the killing of the pig put back to November, in which case feasting might come in for December. If this is so, these bosses at the north end of the east walk of the cloisters might be the end of the series, and the remaining

[1] Rev. E. Venables, *Associated Architectural Reports*, vol. xx, p. 179.

scenes may have been in the north walk which was destroyed when the library was built.

In the nave at Amesbury is a man with a pole-axe killing an ox; the same scene occurs on a misericord at Worcester.

Among grotesque figures of men there is one in the Lincoln cloisters, habited in a cowl, and with wings; he seems to be gazing up at something, but at what it is impossible to say as this part of the boss is missing. At St Mary, Beverley, there are several grotesque figures; in the nave there is a man with no arms or body, his legs spring from his shoulders, and in the north aisle there are two almost identical figures whose arms spring from the sides of the forehead. In the north transept of Bristol Cathedral is a man dressed in a short tunic with a dog's head; dog-headed men were perhaps derived from baboons, and the question as to whether they had souls was debated in the Middle Ages.

Among the most curious of the grotesque figures of men are those just over the windows of the nave in Winchester Cathedral (263–6); most of the window bosses are grotesque figures of beasts, or the heads of men and beasts, but the first two at the east end, on both sides of the nave, are deformed human figures; on the north side over the eastern window the two figures are both human, but with some of the limbs missing, not I think broken off but deliberately left out; one has half of one arm and half of one leg, the other has both arms, but only one leg which ends below the knee; both figures have trumpet-like ears, both are naked and one is holding his genitals in one hand; there is something behind his shoulders which might be meant for short wings. The corresponding figures on the south side too have an appearance of deformity; they both have trumpet-like ears; the first one has horns like a goat's; he has one leg only; the next figure has all its limbs; it has the tips of the fingers of its left hand in its mouth, and on this hand there are six digits. Over the second window from the east, both on the north and the south sides, are beasts with human bodies, the two most easterly figures are rather more human than the westerly; one, a male figure, has two small mammary glands on its breast; it has a grotesque beast's head and talon-like fingers and toes; its opposite number has four small mammary glands on its breast; it has a bull-like head, and cloven hooves for hands and feet; the next two figures are less human still. After this, going west, there are no more of these abortive figures. Over the fourth window on the south side there is a rather nice little figure, naked except for a head-dress rather like that of a chef, who is blowing a trumpet and has his cheeks slightly puffed out.

There are two bosses in the nave at Worcester, also over windows, of misshapen human beings; both are in a crouching attitude; one has talon-like fingers and toes (287), the other has a cloven hoof for one hand, the feet not being visible; one is phallic.

Men are found performing various actions; there are examples of men wrestling at Lincoln (132), in the Angel quire, at Exeter, Norwich cloisters, Lechlade, and two at St Mary, Beverley; these figures lack all appearance of action; an attempt is made in some cases to represent one wrestler as trying to trip up his opponent, but the representation is anything but lifelike. Several examples are interesting because they clearly show the girdle, the band that wrestlers used to wear; it passed over one shoulder and under the opposite arm.

At Exeter there is a man with a large roundish object balanced on the palm of his right hand, and he is poised as though about to throw it; is it meant for putting-the-weight, or is it David hurling a stone at Goliath? In the cloisters at Lacock there are several amusing bosses; on one an acrobat is jumping over a staff that he holds in his hands; on another a tumbler has bent so far forward that he has his head between his legs and is looking out backwards; on yet another a man is looking through what appears to be a horse-collar while a dog is barking at him. In the nave of St Mary, Beverley, a man is scaring birds (27).

Relatively few men are to be found with musical instruments; these are left principally to angels. In the north aisle of the nave at Winchester is a man playing the bagpipes (260), and there is another in the cloisters at Wells. There are several examples of a man blowing a double horn, as in the south aisle of the nave at Winchester, in the nave at St Mary, Beverley, and in the cloisters at Lincoln. At Croscombe a man plays a harp and another a tabor, the latter too appears to be dancing. In the cloisters at Norwich a woman beats a tabor while a man plays on a wind instrument, blowing his cheeks out in the process. In the south aisle of the nave at Winchester there is a man playing on a double pipe; he is surrounded by sheep; in one of the angles of the vaulting-ribs there is a head and a hand holding a scroll; if this is meant for an angel, the whole composition may be connected with the Nativity, though no other boss in the long series in the nave aisles at Winchester is connected with scenes from the life of Christ. In the cloisters at Wells there is a man playing on a pipe. In the cloisters at Norwich there is a boss with two men sitting on horses that have human heads; one man is blowing a very long trumpet, the other has a viol. Among the bosses over the windows of the nave at Winchester are two figures playing on trumpets.

In the quire at Exeter is a man riding on a goat; he is naked except for a net over his shoulders; he holds the horn of the goat in one hand and its tail in the other; he is riding face to head but is looking back over his right shoulder.

Sometimes men are fighting; in the cloisters at Norwich two men are fighting with swords. In the same cloisters a man and a woman are having a violent fight, a scene that is more full of action than is usual; the man is stepping over a square board which may be an overturned table, or may be, as has been suggested,[1] a chess-board, and that the man and woman are quarrelling over a game, though the action suggests some more serious trouble.

A boss in the Norwich cloisters shows a woman giving birth to a child (145); several figures stand round, two with crowns; a central figure standing on a rock probably represents St Michael, but it is much mutilated; the story, found in the *Golden Legend*[2] tells how a woman with child went with a great company of people to St Michael's Mount and in crossing the sands was caught by the tide, but 'St Michael kept the wife whole, and she was delivered and childed among the waves in the middle of the sea'.[3]

It is not possible to enumerate the many figures and demi-figures of men and women that are to be found on roof bosses, especially on the later ones. Many such figures may be studied at St Mary, Beverley, where there are quite a number of figures, grotesque and otherwise. Among the less grotesque are several men in short tunics, some in waist-bands, one is standing in the middle of a wreath. Among the grotesque figures (21–4) are two of naked men, one pursued by a nondescript beast with a head at each end of its body, the other standing before an equally nondescript figure with a human body but the head of a beast with a single short horn; the beast is holding a long staff. There is a man holding a bowl and a flagon and there is a coiled two-legged beast below; I suggest that this boss is meant to represent drunkenness. There is another boss on which two figures are represented, a man and a woman, clothed only in their shifts; they stand facing one another, and the woman carries a bowl. Near the west end of the nave there is a naked woman, and on the boss immediately opposite is the phallic figure of a man.

Before leaving the subject of human figures attention must be called to two bosses in the ninth bay of the south aisle of the nave at Winchester. One represents the demi-figure of a bearded man wearing a cloak with a hood which,

---

[1] *Norwich Cathedral Cloister*, p. 5.　　　　　　　　　[2] Vol. v, p. 183 (Temple Classics).
[3] This is not a miracle of the Virgin as stated in *Norwich Cathedral Cloister*, under boss F. G. 96.

however, is turned back leaving the head bare (258); the man is clutching the cloak with both hands as though drawing it across him to keep out the cold. On a neighbouring boss is another demi-figure with a short beard; he has a hood over his head, a scalloped collar, with buttons down the front of both collar and tunic, and also on the sleeves; he is apparently fastening a belt round his waist. Both figures, especially the first, are very pleasing and lifelike.

In only one instance has a skull been noted on roof bosses; this is in the south crypt in Glasgow Cathedral; the skull is surrounded by trefoil foliage, and two worms are shown on the forehead.

CHAPTER V

HEADS

The subject of heads is an immense one; we find single heads and groups of heads everywhere; except foliage, they form the most numerous type of bosses, and, in a work such as this, one can only deal with the most salient features. One may perhaps divide them into various classes: religious, ecclesiastics, kings, queens, men, women, and beasts.

The head of Christ occurs fairly often and can generally be recognized by having a cross-bearing nimbus, or by wearing the Crown of Thorns. Among the former there are two at Exeter, one in the Lady Chapel, and one in the chapel of St Paul. Others occur at Christ Church, Oxford, Melrose, in the south aisle of the nave at Winchester, and at St Mary, Beverley, in the chancel and in its south aisle. The head of Christ wearing the Crown of Thorns occurs in the Lady Chapel at Ely, in St Stephen's Cloisters, Westminster, and in the south aisle of the nave at Winchester.

There are heads with neither cross-bearing nimbus nor the Crown of Thorns which are nevertheless probably meant for the head of Christ; there is one example at Meavy (135).

Of ecclesiastics I have found four heads of popes. One is in the quire at Exeter, c. 1300, where the head and shoulders are shown, and the pope's hands are raised as though supporting the vaulting-ribs; the old form of papal tiara is shown which in Rome gave place to the triple tiara at about this time. In the nave of the same Cathedral is another head of a pope (102), c. 1350, and here too the old form of tiara is worn; this figure must be meant for John XXII, though one can hardly suppose that it is a portrait.[1] The other two heads of popes are both shown in the modern form of triple tiara, one is at Beaulieu in Hampshire, the other at Burwell (46).

Of ordinary mitred heads there are a great number; most of them are probably meant for bishops, though some may be meant for mitred abbots. One of the earliest is in the quire at Exeter, c. 1300, where the bishop, like the

[1] Grandison had been his chaplain at Avignon, and after his appointment as Bishop of Exeter he corresponded with him and visited him at Avignon in 1331.

pope mentioned above, is supporting the vaulting-ribs with his gloved and ringed hands. In the north transept of Bristol Cathedral there is a group of three mitred heads, the chin of one touching the tip of the mitre of the next. In the nave at Amesbury, besides the head of a bishop, is one of a cardinal; these bosses are probably early sixteenth century, and it is possible that the cardinal may be meant for Campeggio who was appointed to the see of Salisbury in 1524 by Pope Clement VII and with Wolsey was to adjudicate on the divorce of Henry VIII; or it may of course be meant for Wolsey himself.

The only monk's heads that I have come across are doubtful ones in the cloisters at Canterbury. There are very few heads of priests; in the FitzAlan Chapel at Arundel there are three or four, recognizable as priests because they are wearing amices. At St Helen, Norwich, there is a head with what seems to be an almuce, and so is presumably a priest, but this exhausts the list of heads which can definitely be identified with priests, though it is quite possible that many other heads may be meant for priests.

There are a great number of kings' heads as might be expected; I have recorded forty. Probably the earliest is in the quire at Exeter, c. 1300; it is the head of an elderly man with a beard and is perhaps meant for Edward I, though it can hardly be a portrait. Another head of a king comes in a slightly later part of the quire, and has been attributed to Edward II, but if it was meant for him it must be entirely a fancy portrait, for at the date when the boss was carved Edward II must have been a young man, whereas this head is that of a stout middle-aged man.

It would be tedious to go through the list of the heads of kings; no doubt such heads must have been meant for that of the king reigning at the time, but it is unlikely that they were in any sense of the word portraits; they were merely the conventional heads of kings. The only definite exception is the portrait boss of Charles I and his Queen in the vaulting under the tower at Winchester (268), but here we have emerged from medieval times.

What applies to kings' heads applies equally to queens'. The very beautiful head in the fourth bay of the quire at Exeter may be meant for Margaret the second wife of Edward I; the well-carved but slightly unpleasant face of a queen between the fifth and sixth bays may be meant for Isabella the wife of Edward II, and the queen's head in the third bay of the nave may be meant for Philippa the wife of Edward III, but that any of these are portraits is highly improbable.

It is almost impossible to give even a summary of the heads of men, there are so many; bearded, moustached, clean-shaven; some good looking, some very grotesque and often with protruding tongues; some are bare-headed, some have various forms of head-dress. There are two in the Lady Chapel at Exeter which are supposed to be craftsmen, though this is only conjectural; they have bands round their heads whose ends go over the tops of their heads. A negro's head in the Lady Chapel at Ely is so extremely lifelike, with curly hair, flattened nose, and thick lips, that there must have been a negro at Ely in the middle of the fourteenth century (96).

Heads of women are not so common as those of men, but still they are quite numerous; they are found with various kinds of head-dress, veil, reticulated, wimple, horned, pedimental, with a pleated band over the forehead, and one, in Bristol Cathedral, with a band over the nose; this was a fashion that originated in Spain, and was probably derived from the *yashmak* of Moorish women; the fashion apparently spread as far as this country.[1]

At Stratford-sub-Castle in the nave is a woman's head with a gag, in the shape of an oblong block, in her mouth.

Heads with wings are occasionally found. In the Lady Chapel at Ely there is a man's head with a pair of feathered wings which meet over the top of his head (95). In the north aisle of the nave at Gloucester there is a grotesque head of a man with protruding tongue and bat's wings.

There are an extraordinary number of heads with protruding tongues. One in the south aisle at Hereford has the eyes closed, and appears to be dead, possibly hanged. But there are very many where the eyes are not closed and the head cannot be meant for that of a dead man. Such heads are found everywhere in churches of the fourteenth and fifteenth centuries; one may mention the Lady Chapel at Ely and the later work at Canterbury where very many examples may be found. Quite a number of these heads with protruding tongues have foliage from the mouth as described below.

Grotesque heads are very numerous and are to be found all through the Gothic period, though they are comparatively rare early, but extremely common in later times. There are several in the Early English roof at Warmington. There are many in the nave at Canterbury; one of them appears to have the vaulting-ribs growing into its face which has on it an expression of pain and distress (62).

---

[1] See Ruth Matilda Anderson, 'Pleated Headdresses of Castilla and Leon', *Notes Hispanic, the Hispanic Society of America* (1942), p. 51. A particularly fine example occurs on a misericord in Winchester Cathedral.

We find many groups of heads, as in the Norman boss in the Treasury at Canterbury (5), where there are four heads chin to chin. At Boxgrove there are eight heads on one boss (300), forehead to forehead with only eight eyes between them, each face sharing an eye with its neighbour, and in the south aisle of the quire at Chichester there is a rather similar group of six heads; in the same aisle there is another group of six heads, but here the eyes are twelve in number, none being shared between neighbours. At Havant, where the two bosses show a Chichester influence, there is one with four heads forehead to forehead. In the north aisle of the nave at Canterbury (64) there is a boss with one head on one side of it, and two on the other, the two heads share an eye between them so that there are only three eyes. In the chapter-house at Elgin there are three bosses each having two heads, each pair of heads sharing a fore-head between them. In the south crypt at Glasgow there is a boss having four heads chin to chin, the two opposite each other are kings, the other two women; all have their eyes closed. Many more groups of heads might be cited, but mention must be made of two sets of four each, men and women alternately with intertwining foliage in the quire at Exeter. These two are the most pleasing of all the head groups that have come to my notice.

Amongst other curious heads are those known as 'toothache' figures; in these the mouth is held open by the two hands. There is one in the south quire aisle at Canterbury, but I am under the impression that this is an insertion and is considerably later than the late twelfth century when the aisle was built. The earliest examples of which I am sure are in the cloisters and in the entrance to the cloisters at Lincoln, dating from the end of the thirteenth century. There are three fourteenth-century examples in the north aisle of the nave at Winchester, and two more in the high vault, in bosses just over the windows. There are a few examples elsewhere. Though they are popularly known as 'toothache' figures I very much doubt whether this is their real meaning, though I have no alternative explanation.

Of beasts also there are a great number of heads. The earliest probably are a beast's in the north aisle of the nave at Peterborough (178) and two beasts' heads with that of a man at Tickencote (1). It is very often difficult to say what beast the head is meant to represent; and indeed it is sometimes not possible to say if a head is meant to be that of a beast or the grotesque head of a man. A certain number are definitely lions, as in the south and north walks of the Norwich cloisters, in the Black Prince's chantry at Canterbury, in the south transept at Hexham, in the chancel of St Mary, Bury St Edmunds, though even with these some imagination must be used. But if one takes the numerous beasts' heads in the nave of Canterbury, for instance, it is hardly possible to put a name to any of them. At St Mary, Bury St Edmunds, a cow is recognizable, and another beast has possibly a ring through its nose and may therefore be supposed to be a bull.

Many heads of beasts are definitely grotesque and were probably not meant for any particular animal. Amongst these there are two at St Mary, Leicester, one crowned and another wearing a mitre.

Mention has been made in Chapter 1 of the heads that occur so frequently with leaves sprouting from the mouth (300-19). The earliest examples in this country occur in Norman work, but not actually on Norman bosses; there is a very good specimen on the carving on the south doorway of Kilpeck Church in Herefordshire. Perhaps the earliest boss with this motif is at Boxgrove Priory (300), where on one boss there are eight heads with only eight eyes between them, each head sharing an eye with its neighbours; every alternate head has a small stem proceeding from the mouth and disappearing under the chin. In the south aisle of the quire at Chichester there is a rather similar boss of about the same date, first half of the thirteenth century, of six heads; from the mouth of each two large leaves protrude. In New Shoreham there are heads in the angles of the vaulting-ribs with stems growing out of the mouth and spreading, with leaves, over the lower surface of the boss, so that from immediately below the boss appears as though merely carved with foliage. At Blyth Priory there is exactly the same arrangement.

In the curious Early English wooden roof at Warmington, Northamptonshire, built, like the cloisters at Lincoln, to imitate stone vaulting, are a number of foliate heads (302, 303); and here we get a variation of the motif that became commoner at a later date; some of the heads have foliage growing out of the mouth, but one has it growing out of the nostrils, and another out of the eyes.

The foliate head grows commoner as time goes on and there are hundreds of examples on bosses of the fourteenth and fifteenth centuries. In the quire of Ely, the work of Alan de Walsingham, most of the bosses are foliage, but on four of them are leafy faces (309), and from the floor it is impossible to distinguish them from pure foliage except on the very brightest days, and even then it is doubtful whether they would be detected at all unless one knew they were there and they were especially looked for. In the Lady Chapel at Ely (310, 311) there are very many such heads, and on one the leaves cover the face entirely so that only the eyes are visible.[1] There is, or was, a very similar head in the church of St Sebaldus at Nuremburg.

The way the foliage comes from the mouth is very varied. In the south aisle of the nave at Winchester (314) is a face with large leaves coming from each corner of the mouth, and two similar leaves coming from the base of the forehead just above the nose; another has an oak-stem coming from the mouth with two acorns hiding all the mouth except the upper lip; another has two leaves growing out of the chin and others from the forehead, the face itself not being hidden at all; yet another has leaves from the mouth, from the corner of the eyes and from the forehead.

In the wooden bosses of the wagon roofs of the West country one finds endless examples, some extremely well carved, some of very inferior workmanship. At Sampford Courtenay (316) there is an extremely fine bearded head with a stem coming from each side of a half-open mouth with a large leaf partly hiding the beard; the two branches curve upward on each side of the face to meet above the forehead. In the West country are quite a number of faces with a stem or leaves coming from one side of the mouth only, as at South Tawton.

Though the majority of the foliate heads are those of men, we sometimes find women as well, but they are much rarer. But of beasts with mouth foliage we find a large number, most of them heads, but occasionally the whole beast is shown, as the dragon in the south quire aisle at Exeter, the wolf at Tewkesbury, and the dragon on the screen in the retroquire in Beverley Minster.

One expects to find foliate heads in nearly all collections of fifteenth-century bosses, and as already mentioned one finds many earlier examples as well. It would be tedious to mention many examples, but it may be noted here that on the high vault of Pershore Abbey (319) and in Rochester Cathedral there are exceptionable numbers. Under the tower at Salisbury there are a great number of bosses, all except one being foliage, but that one is a head with mouth foliage.

Sometimes the heads are grotesque (313), sometimes they have a look of pain or discomfort, and no wonder! Some are evil-looking, but some are not in the least of this type; they may be quite good-looking and placid (312).

Connected perhaps with such sprouting heads are figures with the lower half hidden in a leafy cylinder or some other shaped covering of foliage. There are

[1] See C. J. P. Cave, 'The Roof Bosses in Ely Cathedral', *Cambridge Antiquarian Society's Communications*, vol. XXXII (1932), p. 37, and Plate VII, fig. 23.

two such on corbels at the west end of the nave at Tewkesbury; they used to be called Adam and Eve, names which the absence of nudity disproves; now, with no better reason than that one is an old man, the other a young woman, they are called David and Bathsheba; the lower half of each figure is encased in a cylinder of conventional foliage. There are some rather similar figures at Ely on bosses at the base of the lantern; each figure is crowned, six are men, and two probably women. They all have the lower half of the body covered with foliage. At Exeter there is a figure of a woman with the lower half hidden in a large mass of foliage; with one hand she clasps a stem in exactly the same way as does the queen in the Ely octagon.

Many of these figures recall the Jack-in-the-Green which was a familiar figure on May Day in England fifty years ago, and which may possibly still survive in some places. Jack-in-the-Green was no doubt a survival of pre-Christian tree worship which had filtered down through the Middle Ages even into the nineteenth century. There can be little doubt that in the Middle Ages such survivals of an ancient cult must have been still more numerous. Tree worship was intimately connected with fertility rites, and Jack-in-the-Green and the rites of the May King are generally held to be so connected.[1] It seems therefore that it is quite a possible suggestion that the sprouting faces and kindred figures may have been intended for fertility figures or charms of some sort by their carvers, which might explain why they are often, but not always, put in obscure places, for if they were charms they might hardly have been looked on with approval by authorities imbued with more orthodox ideas.

Sometimes, though not often, a king is shown with mouth foliage, as in the south transepts at Pershore (318) and Tewkesbury. If the above theory is at all correct, these may represent the King-of-the-May. Another figure, that may be meant as such, is found on the high vault of the quire at Exeter, where a king holding a sceptre appears to be seated on a stem with large oak leaves all round. And in this connection it may be worth noting that a great deal of the foliage, though not all, that appears on these heads and figures is oak, a tree intimately connected with tree worship.

I suggested the connection of these heads and figures with Jack-in-the-Green[2] from the likeness of the boss in the Lady Chapel at Ely to the Jack-in-the-Green

---

[1] See Sir James Frazer, *The Golden Bough* (abridged edition, 1923), p. 129, where Jack-in-the-Green is classed as a relic of tree worship.

[2] 'The Roof Bosses in Ely Cathedral', loc. cit. p. 36.

I used to see as a boy (311). Quite independently Lady Raglan came to the same conclusion as to the origin of what she calls 'the Green Man'.[1]

I have gone into this subject rather fully because these figures have passed almost unnoticed, and those who have noticed them have looked on them as fancies of the carvers. But I consider the motive to be much too definite and that it must have had some meaning that was well known to the sculptor. The May Day festivities, when men dressed up in greenery, were known to all in medieval times, and it seems to me not too far-fetched an idea to connect them with the leafy faces.

[1] Lady Raglan, 'The Green Man in Church Architecture', *Folk-Lore*, vol. L (1939), p. 45.

CHAPTER VI

BEASTS, BIRDS AND FISH

A VERY few Norman bosses have animal carvings; Tickencote has two beasts' heads, besides one human; Iffley, Elkstone and Kilpeck have rather flatly carved beasts' heads (2-4), and there is a beast's head in the north aisle of the nave at Peterborough (178).

When we come to the bosses of the early Gothic period we very soon meet with dragons amid the trefoil foliage (326). We get a few in the late twelfth-century quire aisles at Canterbury, and after that they become quite common; nearly all the large Early English churches have foliage bosses in some of which dragons are to be found; Lincoln (126-9), Salisbury, Westminster, Wells all have examples. In the undercroft at Wells are the heads of a man and a woman with a dragon by each one, and on another boss a seated figure and a dragon; in both cases it looks as though the dragon might be speaking to the man or woman. In the south aisle of the nave at Lincoln is a man's head surrounded by four or five dragons, which seem to be attacking it; two have their claws on its throat. In the muniment room at Westminster we have a centaur and an amphisbaena fighting one another (230), and a man attacked by two dragons. Towards the beginning of the fourteenth century we find dragons with very long ears which are quite typical of the period; there are a number of these at Exeter; in the Bishop's muniment room on a corbel there are two tearing at a man's throat. Dragons fighting with lions are extremely common, examples are at Canterbury, Lincoln, Tewkesbury, Norwich, Winchester, Worcester, York and elsewhere.

Near the west end of the south aisle of the nave at Winchester is the curious subject of a dragon in the courtyard of a castle; at the top is the castle-keep with a central tower and in front of it is a gateway, closed by a portcullis and flanked by two turrets; there is a curtain-wall round the courtyard, with four turrets; the dragon, which is represented as lying on its side, takes up the whole space of the courtyard.

The lion is the most common animal to be found on roof bosses; there are examples in very many churches, but they do not occur as early as dragons and there are not many till the fourteenth century; Exeter has sixteen bosses on which lions appear. Among the few early examples may be mentioned the four lions with one head in common in the chapter-house at Christ Church, Oxford.

Among other animals found on roof bosses are a few apes; at Cley-next-the-Sea two are birching a man; at St Mary, Bury St Edmunds, one holds a urinary flask (55), perhaps a satire on doctors. Bats are found occasionally, there are several at Winchester; perhaps the best is on a wooden boss at Croscombe, Somerset (80). Bears are found occasionally, sometimes chained and muzzled as in the north transept at Ely, and at Blunham; sometimes a bear climbs a pole as at Stratford-sub-Castle (295). Boars and pigs are fairly frequent; in the ambulatory at Exeter are four boars' heads amid naturalistic oak foliage, where they are eating acorns; at Selby a boar stands under an oak tree (195), as it does also at Wootton Courtenay. Sometimes a pig is playing on a musical instrument, such as bagpipes and a harp as at St Mary, Beverley (28). The sow and farrow is fairly common, but I have only found examples in the south and west of England (183). A bull, cow and calf are found together in the Lady Chapel at Exeter; bull-baiting is in the nave aisle at Winchester; in the Canterbury cloisters a bull is tossing a wild man; in the nave at Amesbury an ox is being pole-axed.

Dogs are extremely common; they are often curled up asleep as in the chancel of St Mary, Beverley, the cloisters at Canterbury and Worcester, the screen at Carlisle, and the south aisle of the nave at Tewkesbury. A queen has two lap-dogs at Lincoln (122); two chase rabbits at Exeter; they lick themselves at Carlisle, at Broadclyst, and in the nave at Worcester; they gnaw bones at Sherborne (207) and Walpole St Peter; one attacks a muzzled bear at St Mary, Bury St Edmunds; and one barks at a man looking through a horse-collar at Lacock Abbey. A fox is frequent; it carries off a goose at Lacock, both in the abbey and in the parish church, at St Mary, Beverley, St Mary, Bury St Edmunds, and in the cloisters at Canterbury and Worcester; its depredations are interrupted by an old woman in the Canterbury cloisters, and in the porch of Cley-next-the-Sea; it preaches to the geese at St Mary, Bury St Edmunds (52) and at St Mary, Beverley (25), where, unseen by the geese, it has a dead bird in a sack over its back; one of the geese is silly enough to be bringing an offering in its beak. The fox is tried by the geese in the Canterbury cloisters, where, as well as in the cloisters at Worcester and at St Mary, Bury St Edmunds (53), it is finally hung by the geese. Goats are sometimes found eating vine or other leaves, as in the Norwich and Salisbury cloisters; at Exeter a man, naked except for a net over his shoulders, is riding on a goat.

A hart, sometimes couchant and sometimes chained and gorged, which occurs in a number of places, probably owes its popularity to being a badge of Richard II. Horses are mostly found in connection with men riding them, but there is one by itself in the FitzAlan chapel at Arundel (16), being the badge of the FitzAlan family. A stallion occurs at Sampford Brett and at St Mary, Beverley. Sheep are seen with shepherds in connection with Nativity scenes. In the chapter-house at Chester there is a curious boss of a lamb standing on a dragon; this may have a symbolical meaning, especially as the lamb has the fore-leg bent backwards as in representations of the Agnus Dei, but in this case it carries no banner.

There are a few rabbits or hares, it is difficult to tell which; the most curious are the three rabbits with only three ears between them, each rabbit sharing an ear with its neighbours; this device is found at Broadclyst, North Bovey (49), Chagford, Sampford Courtenay (182), Spreyton, South Tawton, Tavistock, and Widecombe-in-the-Moor, all villages on or not far from Dartmoor; at Selby there is a similar arrangement, but there is a fourth rabbit unconnected with the three.[1]

A squirrel in hazel foliage is at Exeter, and in the Latin Chapel at Christ Church, Oxford; another is eating a nut at Lacock Abbey. A wolf with mouth foliage is on a boss at St Edmund's Chapel at Tewkesbury, a reference evidently to the legend of the wolf guarding the head of St Edmund after he had been decapitated by the Danes.

Besides these beasts there are others which are obviously taken from the medieval bestiaries. The most important of these are to be found on the wooden bosses in the chancel of Queen Camel church in Somerset.[2] Mr Druce considers that these were copied from a Latin manuscript of the twelfth or early thirteenth century. The subjects are: the phœnix; the *Aspido Chelone*, or sea-tortoise to which mariners make fast thinking it to be an island; a merman; a mermaid or siren with a woman's body, wings, and a fish's tail; an amphisbaena, with a second head at the end of its tail; a dragon and doves; the legend of the tiger and the mirror; a tiger; a griffin; a hyena disinterring and eating a

[1] The three rabbits occur in stained glass at Long Melford. The same motif occurs in Paderborn Cathedral in Germany, on a window known as the Hare Window; see Walter Hotz, *Mittelalterliche Groteskplastic* (Leipsig), p. 47 (text), and p. 68 (plate); this window is even mentioned in Baedeker's *Guide to North Germany*.

[2] G. C. Druce, F.S.A., 'Queen Camel Church. Bosses on the Chancel Roof', *Somersetshire Archaeological and Natural History Society, Proceedings*, vol. LXXXIII (1937), p. 89.

corpse; a basilisk; a horned sheep; a mantichora eating a man; a stag treading on a serpent; a lion; an eagle; the legend of the unicorn and the virgin; an antelope with serrated horns; the elephant and castle; the pelican feeding its young.[1]

Beasts and birds in the same style as those at Queen Camel are to be found in other Somerset churches, as at Sampford Brett and Wootton Courtenay. Other beasts probably taken from the bestiaries are to be found in various places; the antelope at Cawston, Old Cleeve, and Widecombe-in-the-Moor; the elephant and castle at Lacock Abbey and Selby (194); the hyena eating a corpse at St Mary, Beverley. A unicorn is among the Creation bosses in the nave at Norwich. An animal which does not figure at Queen Camel, but which frequently comes into the bestiaries, is the panther; the legend about it was that its breath was so sweet-smelling that every animal was attracted to it except the dragon which was repelled, and the panther is made an emblem of Christ. In the chapel of St Edmund at Tewkesbury (219) is a representation of a panther surrounded by nine other beasts who all have their snouts close up to the panther; they include an ape, a ram, a goat and a horse; there is also a wild man, that is a man with shaggy hair over his body.

At Meavy (134) is a grotesque head with large ears, in one of which is a mouse; in the other ear the mouse's tail can be seen, symbolizing perhaps someone with an empty head.

There are not so many birds on roof bosses as there are beasts, but there are still a great number. In many cases it is not possible to tell what species is intended, and they can only be described under the general heading of birds, like those eating fruit among foliage in the ambulatory at Exeter. Of birds that can be put down to real species by far the most common is the eagle. Some of these are evidently intended for the symbol of St John the Evangelist; indeed, whenever an eagle appears carrying a label or with one close to it this may be suspected. But apart from these we find a great many eagles. In Exeter we have one pecking the eyes out of a lion, another feeding on a pig, and four eagles feeding on the carcass of a cow. In the south aisle of the nave at Winchester an eagle is carrying off a sheep, and at St Mary, Beverley, Wootton Courtenay, and Worsted an eagle is preying on another bird. At Bicknoller three are chasing a lion. At Lichfield an eagle is pecking at a lamb that has apparently a pack on its back.

---

[1] Those wishing to know the legends connected with these beasts should consult Mr Druce's paper, loc. cit.

There are a number of double-headed eagles, chiefly in Devon and Cornwall; for example, Chagford, Lifton, St Madron, Morwenstowe, South Tawton; there is also one in the chancel of St Mary, Beverley, and another in the south transept at Amesbury. The double-headed eagle has been supposed to have some relation to Richard Earl of Cornwall, second son of King John, who was elected Emperor of the Holy Roman Empire, but this seems a far-fetched idea seeing that there were numerous families in this country who bore the double-headed eagle on their coat of arms. In Papworth's *British Armorials* there are over a hundred entries under this charge.

Geese are mostly associated with the fox as noticed above. An owl with a mouse in its beak is found at Cley-next-the-Sea, St Mary, Bury St Edmunds, and at Lacock Abbey. Owls are sometimes represented being mobbed by small birds; examples are at Exeter, Sherborne (206), and in the cloisters at Norwich and Wells.

Pelicans wounding their breasts, and often with their young in a nest are extremely common. There are some at Winchester where the bird also appears as the charge on the arms of Bishop Fox (252-4). A swan, sometimes chained and collared, occurs several times at Lacock Abbey and once in the parish church; three times at St Mary, Bury St Edmunds; once at Market Harborough, and once in the Creation bosses in the nave at Norwich. There is another very good one on a late wooden boss at Burwell. At Wootton Courtenay there is a swan, chained and collared, with its young on its back, floating on water in which a fish is swimming.

Fish are less common than birds. Three are often found lying one over another so that the head of each one is over the tail of another, a position known in heraldry as *tête à la queue*; they may be meant for armorial bearings; there are examples at Beaulieu, in the north transept at Bristol (30), in the Lady Chapel at Gloucester, and in the quire at Peterborough. In the chancel of St Mary, Beverley, are two fish saltireways, and this too is probably heraldic. At St Madron are three fish side by side, in the position known to heralds as *hauriant*. In the ambulatory at Exeter are four fishes, each one biting the tail of another. There are also fish in the nave of St Mary, Beverley, in the chancel of St Mary, Bury St Edmunds, and at Lacock, both in the abbey and in the parish church. Three fish at Selby are probably modern. At Ockham there is a fish-trap made of wicker-work and corded, with a fish swimming into it. None of these fish is very correctly represented and in general it is not possible to say what kinds are intended.[1]

[1] The three fish in the Lady Chapel at Gloucester have the appearance of being real fish, but the late Sir Charles Regan, F.R.S., who examined a photograph, said that they were of no known species.

Insects are extremely rare. In the nave of St Mary, Beverley (26), there is an obvious caterpillar, though it has a head like a dog, and in the ambulatory at Exeter amongst the naturalistic foliage is a boss with three creatures which are almost certainly meant for caterpillars. In the north aisle of the chancel of St Mary, Beverley, are two creatures with wings that must be meant for insects; they have jointed bodies and their heads are seemingly meant for insects' heads.

The only molluscs I have come across are a snail in the Lady Chapel of Lacock Church, and another in the midst of foliage in the chancel of St Mary, Bury St Edmunds; this is a conical shell and is very well portrayed.[1]

Besides real animals there are a number of fabulous beasts some of which have been mentioned in connection with Queen Camel. Centaurs are fairly common and are found both early and late in the Gothic period. In the muniment room at Westminster Abbey (230) is the extremely fine boss with a centaur, half-man and half-lion, fighting with an amphisbaena. There is another centaur in the Abbey (228), in the south aisle of the nave, half-man and half-horse; he is about to shoot an arrow from a bow as he gallops along. In the nave at Exeter is a bearded centaur holding a spear. In the tower at Lincoln two centaurs are fighting with sword and target. In the north-east transept at Beverley Minster a centaur is standing before a dragon and is aiming an arrow at it. In the north transept of Bristol Cathedral (31) are two curious beings that may perhaps be classed with centaurs; both have the heads and bodies of women, but from the waist downward they are beasts; they differ from the ordinary centaur in having only two legs, one almost certainly a lion's, the other indeterminate. In the Lady Chapel at Gloucester is a centaur of whose body one can only say that it has a long tail; the man part has a grotesque head, has a sword in one hand, and is holding his tail in the other. On one of the wooden bosses in the quire at Peterborough is a centaur with the body of a lion; he holds a scimitar in one hand and a heater-shaped shield in the other, and wears a cap rather like a cap of liberty; he is clothed in a long tunic which is draped over the fore-part of the lion's body. In the nave of St Mary, Beverley, is a centaur with a bird perching on his left hand.

Among fabulous beings mermaids are very numerous. Perhaps the best example of all is on an early fourteenth-century boss in the quire at Exeter (100); here the mermaid is holding her own tail; in the chapel of St Paul at Exeter is

---

[1] There is a snail on the string-course below the windows in the south aisle of Great St Mary's Church, Cambridge.

another mermaid who holds her tail in one hand and a fish in the other. Mermaids are often shown holding a comb in one hand and a mirror in the other; perhaps the best example is in the nave at Sherborne (204); others are at the deanery, Carlisle, Croscombe, Lacock cloisters, two examples, Newcastle, St Mary, Redcliffe (41), Selby (199), where the mermaid is combing her hair, Stoodleigh, four examples, all very crudely carved (294), Stratford-sub-Castle, Worcester cloisters, two examples. A mermaid is generally represented as a naked woman down to her hips with a fish's body and tail in the place of legs, but at St Mary, Beverley, there is one whose head alone is human, all the rest being a fish. In the cloisters at Canterbury there is a mermaid who seems to have a double tail. Mermaids are sometimes accompanied by mermen; there is an example in the nave of Beverley Minster. In the south transept at York the mermaid is combing her hair and the merman is holding the mirror; the merman in this case has a second pair of fore-limbs which end in a sort of paddle. In the north transept of Bristol Cathedral a mermaid and a merman are holding a crown between them, and in the cloisters at Salisbury the pair hold a wreath between them. A winged mermaid or siren is found at Queen Camel and in the Lincoln cloisters.

Mermen apart from mermaids occur occasionally; there is a good one at Queen Camel, with long hair, and a long beard which the merman holds in one hand while he holds his tail in the other. Mermen fighting with men occur in the muniment room at Westminster, and in the north aisle of the Angel quire at Lincoln (133).

The Signs of the Zodiac occur on the vaulting of the FitzJames' gateway at Merton College, Oxford (174-7). The bosses are very late, c. 1500, but they are remarkably good; the lion and the bull are excellent, and the crab is extremely lifelike, but the scorpion, though well carved, is like nothing in the animal kingdom.[1] The virgin wears a turban and has a very tightly laced dress with wide sleeves; the archer is a centaur. In the centre of the vaulting are the royal arms, France modern and England quarterly, supported by a greyhound and a dragon; half of a rose appears from behind the shield, and above all is a large crown.

The Signs of the Zodiac are reported on bosses round a well-hole under the tower of All Saints, Hastings.

[1] Eight of these bosses are illustrated in the City of Oxford volume of the Royal Commission on Historical Monuments, but Scorpio, which is one of those illustrated, is wrongly attributed to Cancer.

CHAPTER VII

FOLIAGE, FLOWERS
AND MISCELLANEOUS OBJECTS

As FAR AS Norman roof bosses with foliage are concerned the material available is very scanty. In the chapter-house at Bristol and in the entrance thereto are bosses with whorls of petal-like objects; these may be meant for flowers or they may be purely conventional patterns. In the south aisle of the quire at Christ Church, Oxford, there is a quatrefoil leaf pattern, and though it appears on the intersection of Norman vaulting-ribs I should hesitate to attribute it with certainty to Norman times. Besides these and some poor bosses under the Water Tower at Canterbury I have discovered nothing else of Norman date.

It is at Canterbury that we can really begin the study of foliage sculpture on roof bosses. The earlier bosses in the quire erected under William of Sens are either rather simple leaf patterns or rich and elaborate foliage (320, 321), stiff leaves radiating out from the centre with their tips bent backwards towards the edge of the boss, or in one case bent forwards rather like the volutes on the capitals; the foliage reminds one of the acanthus leaves of the capitals, and like them they are deeply divided, so that they become almost a stem with leaves of a trefoil character growing out on each side, and in fact become almost a spray, albeit a very stiff one; Professor Prior says [1] that English leaf-carving shows a different weaving from that on the Continent, 'one essential quality of this being in our habitual rejection of the leaf in favour of the spray as the basis of design'. The midrib on these bosses is very strongly marked; it is a deep groove that seems almost to cut the leaf in half longitudinally. One boss belonging to this period, in the south-east transept, has the leaves arranged spirally instead of radially with very good artistic effect. This boss and the one east of the Agnus Dei have small holes drilled through the leaves, a method of ornamentation not usually found till the Perpendicular period. [2] In the four bosses at the east end of the quire, erected six years later under William the Englishman, we find the spray and the trefoil foliage fully developed (322, 323). The latter is termed

[1] Edward Prior, *A History of Gothic Art in England*, p. 136.
[2] See Samuel Gardner, *English Gothic Foliage Sculpture*, p. 42.

trefoil for convenience, though here as well as elsewhere some of the leaves have four or five lobes.

The trefoil bosses at Lincoln have already been mentioned (Chapter 1). These leaves bear no resemblance to those at Canterbury. They begin with long straggling leaves in St Hugh's quire and we find a progressive evolution as time went on as though a local style had gradually altered through perhaps three generations of craftsmen (328-31).

Elsewhere[1] I have given full details of the foliage and other bosses at Lincoln. A note may be added that several of the bosses in the nave have small holes drilled in the foliage as in two of the bosses at Canterbury mentioned above.

Southwark Cathedral has five bosses in the quire which must certainly be old, though the vaulting was rebuilt about 1820. The four eastern bosses have very unusual foliage, the leaves are deeply divided and look rather like seaweed (324), and none of it conforms in the least to the conventional trefoil foliage; some of these bosses have angle heads which are not common in this country. The fifth boss is in a different style (325), its foliage consists of long straggling leaves with trefoil ends to the lobes. It seems to me to be likely that the four eastern bosses belong to the original roof of the quire and were incorporated in the roof when the vaulting was rebuilt in the early nineteenth century, and that the fifth boss may have come from the original nave, the vaulting of which was some fifty years later; this vaulting fell in 1469, and there are still some remnants from it in a recess in the nave; there may have been more in the early years of last century.

The history of foliage sculpture on roof bosses for more than half a century after 1200 centres on the trefoil motif. Sometimes the foliage is awkward and clumsy as in the quire at New Shoreham, sometimes it is full of artistic vigour as at Salisbury (186-9); and here there is a definite division between the east end of the quire and the rest of the Cathedral; although trefoil foliage makes up their design, the first four bosses are quite unlike the traditional trefoil pattern; in their curves and convolutions they show great simplicity and great beauty, and it seems to me that we can trace here a different hand from those of the carvers of the rest of the bosses in the Cathedral. These other bosses are all extremely good, though they lack the perfection of the first four.

A great deal of trefoil foliage occurs in the quire of Westminster Abbey, both on the high vault and in the aisles; it may be noted here that the marguerite in

[1] *Archaeologia*, vol. LXXXV, p. 23.

the north aisle of the quire and the rose in the east aisle of the north transept
must be comparatively modern; both can be seen to be bolted on; they
were probably put up to replace broken sculptures and they may be made of
wood.

Practically every building whose vaulting was built between 1200 and 1270,
or sometimes even later, has bosses with trefoil foliage. Perhaps among this
wealth of material the pride of place should be given to the two bosses in the
chapel in the Bishop's Palace at Chichester (333); this chapel may have been
built by Bishop Seffrid at the same time as the presbytery;[1] Hannah says that
the two bosses and the corbels were probably retouched after they were
originally worked; I cannot agree; the two bosses can hardly represent any
retouching operation; what we see to-day must be the original carving of the
two roof bosses, but the style is that of a date very much after Bishop Seffrid
(1180–1204); there seems to be no doubt that the chapel was built then, in
which case the bosses must have been left blank and must have been carved
later; in several ways they remind me of some of the bosses in the nave at
Lincoln, work done under Bishop Grosseteste (1235–53), and I should date the
carving of the two bosses in the chapel at Chichester as from 1240 to 1250.
Nor can I agree with Hannah when he says that the corbels and bosses are
'excellent in general effect, but rather indifferent if closely examined, as is
indeed the case with much medieval sculpture'.

It would be tedious to describe all the variations of trefoil foliage that occur
on roof bosses, but mention must be made of a peculiarity of the foliage that
occurs on the bosses in the presbytery at Ely (344), built under Bishop Northwold
(1229–54); here the lobes of the leaves have lumps on them, a peculiarity which
perhaps foreshadows the lumps which are the normal characteristic of much of
the foliage of the Decorated and of the Perpendicular periods. The foliage on
the capitals have the same lumps.[2]

The same lumps are found on a few of the bosses at Salisbury, but they are not
used with the same freedom as at Ely.

Some years after the middle of the thirteenth century a change came over
foliage sculpture; the trefoil style disappears and is replaced by natural foliage
which is often copied with great accuracy. A slight indication of natural foliage
is seen as early as Salisbury; in the south aisle of the quire there is a flower with

[1] Ian C. Hannah, 'Bishop's Palace Chichester', *Sussex Archaeological Collections*, vol. LII, p. 6.
[2] S. Gardner, *English Gothic Foliage Sculpture*, p. 32.

eight petals, naturalistic in style, though it cannot be identified with any definite flower; in the north-east transept there are some broad leaves quite different from the conventional trefoil, and a five-petal flower occurs in the centre of one of the bosses in the chapter-house. But these are all exceptional.

Probably Westminster Abbey is the first place where naturalistic foliage is freely used, in this country at any rate. There is one boss in the quire with long, straggling, much-divided leaves, and in the transepts we find more examples; in the south transept there are examples of oak, maple and ivy, besides more of the long much-divided leaves. But it is in the first four bays west of the crossing that naturalistic foliage is really freely used, though even here some of the bosses have trefoil foliage. Among the natural plants are oak leaves with acorns and leaf galls, yellow water-lily with its flask-shaped seed-pods, ivy, and vine with fruit which looks rather like loganberry but which is meant no doubt for bunches of grapes. One boss has five large flowers with two whorls of petals, no doubt roses, for the few leaves visible are typical rose leaves; there are also several fruits which are probably meant for hips, though they have bracts below them which do not occur in roses. Some bosses have leaves in the natural style which are difficult to identify with real plants; some look rather like pennywort, and others have deeply divided leaves. The bosses in the corresponding aisles conform to the trefoil pattern.

In the high vault and in the aisles of the Angel quire at Lincoln we get very perfect natural leaves (336-9), though some bosses still have trefoil foliage. Here again we get the yellow water-lily, oak with acorns and leaf galls, maple with its winged seed, and hawthorn sometimes with flowers sometimes with the fruit, and the latter so accurately rendered that even the small black tip to the berries is carved. In the north aisle there is one boss with vine leaves and with bunches of grapes that look much more natural than the blackberry-like fruit which does duty for grapes in so many cases here and elsewhere. In the south aisle there are two wrestlers surrounded by foliage (132), oak with acorns and leaf galls on one side and hawthorn with its berries on the other. In the Angel quire too we get leaves in the naturalistic style which cannot, however, be identified with real plants, and there is one boss with leaves like oak but with five-petalled flowers rather like primroses. There are some leaves which are rather like ranunculus, and on one boss there is foliage very like wormwood.

In the ambulatory at Exeter we meet with almost the most faithful copies of natural foliage to be found anywhere. Here we find the rose, a large spray with many flowers with two whorls of petals; oak leaves with boars feeding on the acorns; a mixture of two kinds of leaves, oak and perhaps beech with goats feeding on them, and what appear to be small caterpillars on some of the leaves. We find maple, hazel with nuts, and a plant with pods like a pea, some open and some not yet open, but all of them showing the peas within; the leaves are pinnate with five broad lobes, not really very like the leaves of a pea or vetch, but there are indications of tendrils. There are foliate heads both in the ambulatory and in the Lady Chapel whose mouth foliage seems to be meant for wormwood; there are vine leaves with small compact bunches of grapes and tendrils; in the Lady Chapel is a boss with maple and its winged seeds on one side and hawthorn with its berries on the other. Many of the foliage bosses in the ambulatory have small beasts or birds among the foliage; one has a beast, perhaps a cat, catching a small bird. There are a few examples of naturalistic foliage in the quire aisles, and in the chapel of St Andrew are excellent examples of oak (342) and hawthorn, and in the chapel of St James, now unhappily destroyed, were equally good examples of wormwood and vine (340-1). In the high vault of the quire we have naturalistic foliage in the eastern bays but not in the western. But in the chapel of St Paul we again find naturalistic foliage; the figure of St Paul himself (104) has rose leaves and roses on each side of him. In the chapel of St John the Baptist we have a few bosses with natural foliage and a few with foliage of a later type. This chapel as well as that of St Paul must have been vaulted before the western bays of the quire and just as the natural style was going out.

In the quire of Pershore there is also much natural foliage; oak, hawthorn, ivy, vine, wormwood, maple; it is good but perhaps not quite so good as that at Exeter.

Southwell is famous for the naturalistic foliage on the capitals and on the carvings above the stalls, but the vaulting shows signs of a change of style; the central boss it is true is naturalistic and probably meant for vine, but the leaves have swellings on them, and the side bosses belong to a later style.

Bosses with natural foliage also occur in the Latin Chapel at Christ Church, Oxford, where among other forms arum leaves are portrayed, in the chapter-houses at Wells and York, and in some other places.

In the ordinary way the naturalistic style came to an end somewhere about 1310–20, but it lingered on spasmodically to nearly the end of the Gothic period, though the species represented were generally restricted to oak, rose and vine, and they are not usually nearly such exact copies from nature as those carved in the period between 1265 or 1270 and 1320. Of these late forms vine is one of the commonest; it occurs for instance in the nave at Canterbury(353), under the tower at Bristol Cathedral (354), in the quire of St Mary, Redcliffe (352), and in other places, including some of the wagon roofs of the West country. The single flower of the rose with no stalks or leaves occurs in late times in a number of churches, but cannot be classed as naturalistic, rather it might be called heraldic. Natural roses, however, do occur up to quite late times; there are examples at Canterbury, Windsor, and Worcester. At the little church of Meavy (355) in Devon there are particularly good late examples of natural rose, as well as oak and vine.

A very exceptional case of late naturalistic style is in the arum flowers on one of the bosses near the west end of the north aisle at Westminster.

Early in the fourteenth century a new style of foliage sculpture came into fashion. The new style is well seen in the quire at Ely (345), built after the fall of the central tower in 1322; the foliage is unlike any natural kind; the leaves are long, deeply divided, and undulated, with rather pointed ends, and a slight but probably unintentional likeness to seaweed; they appear to cling closely to the surface of the boss, which they cover almost completely. They form a very marked contrast to the deeply undercut trefoil in the adjoining presbytery.

In the quire, the sacristy and the Berkely Chapel at Bristol Cathedral (348-51) we find bosses with the same kind of foliage but in a much more ornamental style than that of Ely. In the quire itself the leaves are rather flatter; some are deeply divided and some almost round; they have a small raised rim round the edges; the leaves all cling closely to the bosses as in the Ely examples; one boss is carved with very conventional oak leaves, with many raised knobs on each leaf, and a few acorns among them; these cannot be classed as naturalistic. In the sacristy there are foliage bosses rather like those in the quire; all these bosses are extremely decorative.

In the western bays of the quire at Exeter we find foliage bosses in the newer style, long leaves with undulations and swellings, while in the eastern bays we find naturalistic foliage still in use but with traces of the undulations which marked the later style.

The largest collection of foliage bosses in the Perpendicular style is in the nave at Winchester; the leaves have the undulations and lumps that have been noted on the Decorated bosses, but the general effect of the nave bosses is rather poor and very monotonous; there seems to be a great want of originality, and very similar designs are found in all the twelve bays.

The nave at Canterbury is more varied, there being a large number of heads of men and beasts, but the foliage bosses are extremely poor, though perhaps less monotonous than those at Winchester.

There is a tendency for Perpendicular bosses to become square; there are examples in the quire and Lady Chapel at Gloucester, and it is well seen in the wooden bosses in St Andrew Undershaft, and in many other places, particularly in the wagon roofs of West country churches. The foliage in these late bosses is generally rather poor in design and calls for little comment; occasionally we find belated attempts at naturalism.

It is strange that amid all the wealth of foliage that appears on roof bosses, both naturalistic and conventional, there should be hardly anything that can be attributed to a fern; there is one doubtful example in the south aisle of St Sampson, Cornwall.

Various miscellaneous objects occur on roof bosses, and some may be mentioned here.

At St George's Chapel, Windsor, the Cross Naid is depicted several times (280, 281). This cross, which was supposed to contain a relic of the True Cross was looked on as an object of the highest sanctity; it was taken from Wales by Edward I, and in the reign of Edward III it was given to St George's Chapel where it became its most treasured relic. At the east end of the nave is a boss with a large Celtic cross inlaid with jewels, and on another boss, at the east end of the south aisle of the quire, are figures of Edward IV. and Richard Beauchamp, bishop of Salisbury, kneeling on each side of a Celtic cross from which rays of light proceed.[1] One of the angels which surround the east window is holding a cross which seems to be meant to represent the Cross Naid.

The tracery of windows is found four times at St Mary, Redcliffe (40), and twice at Sherborne; most of these represent rose windows. Roof vaulting is also found on several bosses in St Mary, Redcliffe, and on some of these roof bosses are depicted in the shape of small roses, and what is still more remarkable a boss in the east aisle of the north transept depicts vaulting which is an actual model of the vaulting in the transept (37).

[1] See *Report of the Society of the Friends of St George's* (Dec. 1943), p. 5.

St Mary, Redcliffe, has an example of a maze (36); there is another, but not nearly so good a one, at South Tawton; both mazes are unicursal, that is, there is only one path which when followed leads inevitably to the centre.

In the cloisters at Norwich is a boss with a representation of a half-open door under an ogee arch; the points of a raised portcullis can be made out. A door-knocker is represented in the north aisle of the nave at St Mary, Bury St Edmunds; it is in the shape of the head of a beast with a large ring between its teeth; it can only be meant for a door-knocker.

A set square and compasses occur on a shield in the quire at Peterborough, but they may perhaps be meant for heraldic charges.

In St George's Chapel, Windsor, are a number of representations of a hemp bray (283), the badge of Sir Reginald Bray who was so much concerned with the building of the chapel. There is another representation at Ockham. Such punning rebuses are found fairly frequently. At Canterbury in the north transept we find three gilded stones under a mitre for Prior Goldstone, and a bird perched on an ox which bears the letters N E for Priory Oxney. At Sherborne there are several bosses with a ram and the letters S A M on a scroll for Abbot Ramsam (208). In the quire at Norwich are a large number of bosses with the mouth of a well for Bishop Goldwell. In Bishop Langton's chantry at Winchester are the letters L G on a ton for Langton, and a hen on a ton for Prior Hunton.

Knots have been noted at a number of places, including Windsor, Sherborne, Ockham, Chumleigh, and Lanreath.

In the north transept of Bristol Cathedral are two saddles (32), each with a strap round it, perhaps the girths, though they pass over the top of the saddles; they have quite a modern strap-buckle, and there are holes in the straps for adjusting the length. This is the only example I know of saddles apart from saddles on horses.

Dates are very rare on roof bosses, and the few that occur are all very late. At St Neot, Cornwall, is 1593, Warmington 1650, Buckden 1665, Windsor 1528 (275), South Brent 1637, Crewkerne 1784, Winchester College Chapel 1822.

1. Tickencote   2. Iffley

3. Elkstone   4. Kilpeck

5. Canterbury, Treasury
7. Bristol, chapter-house

6. Pershore
8. Bristol, chapter-house

ABERDEEN

9. Arms of the Empire
11. Forman, Archbishop of St Andrews

10. Leon and Castille
12. Douglas, Bishop of Dunkeld

ARUNDEL, FITZALAN CHAPEL

13. Head with wreath of leaves
15. A prophet

14. Head with wreath of flowers
16. White horse badge of FitzAlan

BEVERLEY, ST MARY, CHANCEL

17. Woman's head
19. Athelstan and St John of Beverley

18. Grotesque monster
20. Foliate head

BEVERLEY, ST MARY, NAVE; GROTESQUES

21.   22.

23.   24.

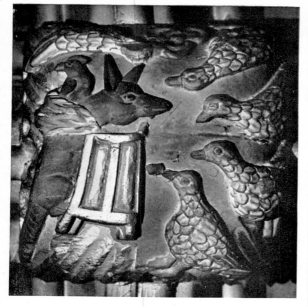

BEVERLEY, ST MARY

25. Lady Chapel; fox preaching to geese

27. Nave; scaring birds

26. Nave; caterpillar

28. Nave; pig and bagpipes

BRISTOL CATHEDRAL, NORTH TRANSEPT

29. Edward II in his death agony
31. Semi-human monster

30. Fish
32. Saddles

BRISTOL ST MARY, REDCLIFFE

33. God the Father   34. God the Son

35. God the Holy Ghost

BRISTOL, ST MARY, REDCLIFFE

36. Maze
38. Woman's head

37. Model of transept roof
39. Man's head

BRISTOL, ST MARY, REDCLIFFE

40. Nave, north aisle; rose window

41. Nave, north aisle; mermaid

42. Tower; man at stool

43. Nave, north aisle; St Katherine, virgin and martyr

44. North Bovey; king's head
46. Burwell; pope's head

45. North Bovey; queen's head
47. Burwell; emperor's head

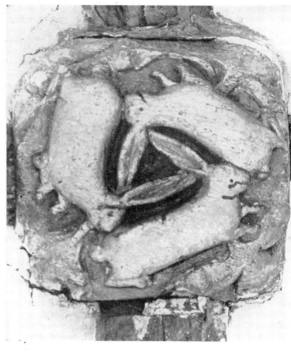

48. Beverley Minster; coronation
50. Blunham; ecclesiastic

49. North Bovey; rabbits
51. Cambridge, Great St Mary; ecclesiastic before crucifix

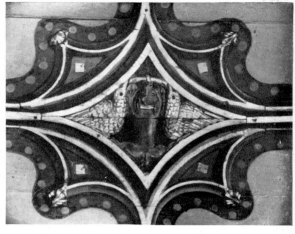

BURY ST EDMUNDS, ST MARY

52. Fox preaching to geese 53. Geese hanging fox
54. Angel with portative organ 55. Ape with urinary flask

56. Brancepeth
58. Broadhembury; man's head

57. Brancepeth
59. Broadhembury; Passion emblems

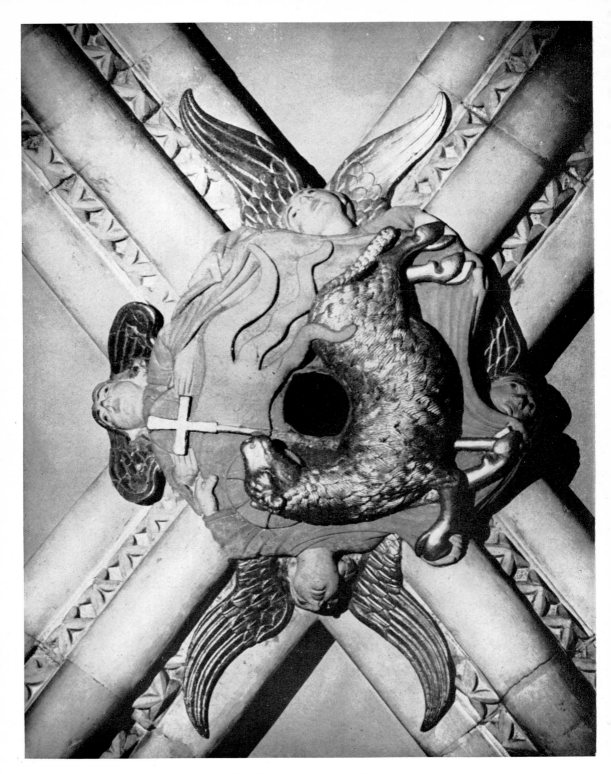

60. Canterbury, centre of quire

CANTERBURY

61. South transept
63. Nave, north aisle

62. Nave
64. Nave, north aisle

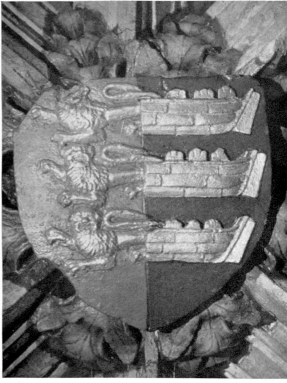

CANTERBURY, CLOISTERS; ARMORIAL

65. Ethiopia   66. Cinque Ports

67. Unknown   68. Stanley

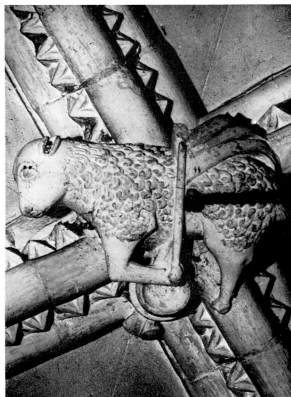

69. Blythburgh; angels
71. Chester, Lady Chapel; Trinity

70. Crondall; Agnus Dei
72. Chester, Lady Chapel; Virgin and Child

CONGRESBURY

73. Foliate Head

74. Old man's head

75. Letter M crowned

76. Geometrical design

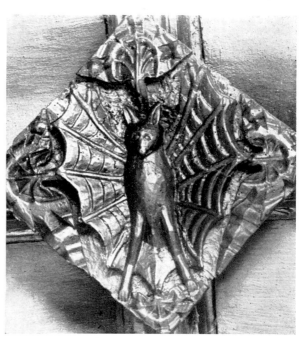

CROSCOMBE

77. Christ in Glory

79. Man with shears

78. Woman with spindle

80. Bat

DURHAM

81. Agnus Dei
83. Foliage and beasts

82. Souls of the just in Abraham's bosom
84. Foliage, beasts and human figures

ELY

85. Presbytery; Coronation
87. Presbytery; a Saint?

86. Presbytery; St Etheldreda
88. Lantern; Christ

ELY, LADY CHAPEL

89. Virgin and Child
91. Assumption

90. Crucifixion
92. Translation of St Etheldreda

ELY, LADY CHAPEL

93. Grotesque; 'toothache'   94. Woman's head
95. Man's head, winged   96. Negro

EXETER, QUIRE

97. Crucifixion   98. Coronation
99. Viol player   100. Mermaid

EXETER

101. Nave; King David

103. Nave; Bishop Grandison

102. Nave; a pope's head

104. Chapel; St Paul

GLOUCESTER, QUIRE; ANGELS

105. With Passion emblems
107. With bagpipes

106. With Passion emblems
108. With portative organ

GLOUCESTER, QUIRE; ANGELS

109. With harp
111. With buzine

110. With symphony
112. With shawm

113. St Just-in-Roseland
115. King's Nympton

114. St Just-in-Roseland
116. King's Nympton

LICHFIELD, QUIRE

117. Last Judgement
119. Annunciation

118. Trinity
120. Assumption

121. Lincoln, Angel quire, aisle; Coronation of the Virgin

LINCOLN, ANGEL QUIRE, AISLES

122. Queen with pet dogs   123. Jesse Tree

124. Prophet and Apostle   125. David and Nathan

LINCOLN, ANGEL QUIRE, AISLES

126. Man and monster fighting
128. Three monsters

127. Winged monster
129. Two winged monsters

LINCOLN, ANGEL QUIRE, AISLES

130. Man and woman kissing
132. Wrestlers

131. Two women's heads
133. Man and merman fighting

MEAVY

134. Head with mouse in ear	135. Head of Christ
136. Typical West country spiral design	137. Typical West country foliage design

NORWICH, CLOISTERS

138. Revelation i. 12–16
140. Fall of Babylon

139. Worship of the Lamb
141. Revelation xvi. 13

NORWICH, CLOISTERS

142. Herod's feast

144. Edward the Confessor's vision

143. Penance of Henry II

145. Miracle of St Michael

NORWICH, NAVE

146. Creation of Eve   147. The Fall
148. Lamech kills Cain   149. Noah builds the Ark

NORWICH, NAVE

150. Noah's Ark

151. Moses in the basket

152. Pharaoh in the Red Sea

153. Jacob peels the rod

NORWICH, NAVE

154. Joseph cast into the pit
156. Samson and the gates of Gaza
155. Joseph and the corn sacks
157. Solomon

NORWICH, NAVE

158. Annunciation

159. Nativity

160. Nailing to the Cross

161. Crucifixion

NORWICH, NAVE

162. Harrowing of Hell
164. Last Judgement

163. Ascension
165. The Trinity

NORWICH, ST HELEN

166. Nativity   167. Ascension

168. Woman's head   169. Man's head

OTTERY ST MARY

170. St Anne and the Virgin   171. Annunciation
172. Virgin and Child   173. Coronation

MERTON COLLEGE, OXFORD; SIGNS OF THE ZODIAC

174. Taurus   175. Leo

176. Virgo   177. Scorpio

PETERBOROUGH

178. North aisle; Norman boss

180. Porch; Trinity

179. Nave, west end

181. Porch; Assumption

SAMPFORD COURTENAY

182. Rabbits
184. Bearded head

183. Sow and farrow
185. Queen's head

SALISBURY

186. Quire, east end

187. Quire, east end

188. Quire, west end

189. Nave, north aisle

SALLE

190. Shepherds at Bethlehem
192. Triumphal entry

191. Circumcision
193. Resurrection

SELBY

194. Elephant and castle   195. Boar

196. Eagle   197. Naturalistic foliage

SELBY

198. Man riding ass

199. Mermaid

200. Triple face

201. Ape

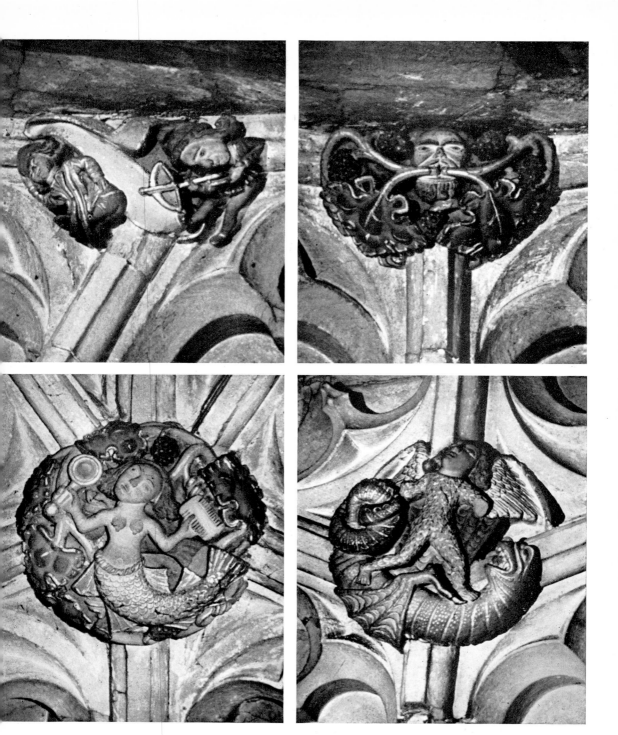

SHERBORNE

202. Man with crossbow 203. Foliate head
204. Mermaid 205. St Michael

SHERBORNE

206. Owl mobbed by small birds

207. Dogs gnawing bones

208. Rebus of Abbot Ramsam

209. Arms of the Abbey

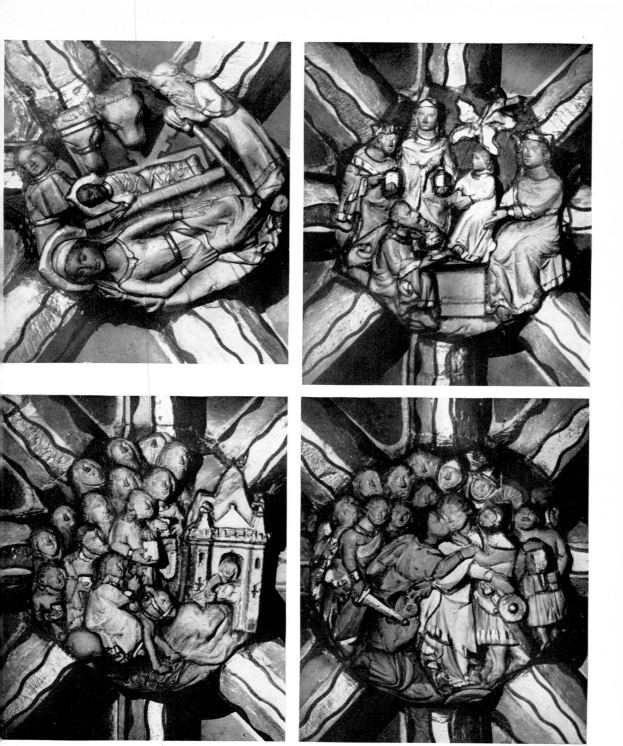

TEWKESBURY, NAVE

210. Nativity   211. Epiphany
212. Triumphal entry   213. Betrayal

TEWKESBURY, NAVE

214. Crucifixion   215. Resurrection
216. Pentecost   217. Coronation

TEWKESBURY

218. South transept; star
220. St Edmund's Chapel; Martyrdom of St Edmund

219. St Edmund's Chapel; panther
221. St Edmund's Chapel; Resurrection

WESTMINSTER, CHOIR OF ANGELS

222. Angels with crown and musical instrument
224. Angels with sundial and pipes

223. Angels with palm branches
225. Angels with book and perhaps host

WESTMINSTER, AISLES

226. Annunciation

228. Centaur with bow

227. Human head and lions

229. Grotesque face

230. Westminster, muniment room

WESTMINSTER

231. Henry VII's Chapel; pendant

233. Henry VII's Chapel, aisle; pendant

232. Chapel of Our Lady of the Pew; Assumption

234. Henry VII's Chapel, aisle; pendant

WESTMINSTER, ST STEPHEN'S CLOISTERS

235. Castle

237. I H S

236. Arms of Wolsey

238. Figure rising from a rose

WINCHESTER, QUIRE; PASSION EMBLEMS

239. Cross   240. The five wounds
241. Vernicle   242. Pillar of the Scourging

WINCHESTER, QUIRE; PASSION EMBLEMS

243. Spear, sponge, loin cloth   244. Malchus
245. Spitting Jew   246. Judas's money-bag

WINCHESTER, QUIRE; ROYAL ARMS

247. Henry VII

249. Henry VIII as Prince of Wales

248. Henry VII

250. Katherine of Aragon

WINCHESTER, QUIRE

251. Tudor badge
253. Exeter impaling Fox

252. Winchester impaling Fox
254. Durham impaling Fox

WINCHESTER

255. Lady chapel; Christ in Glory
257. Nave aisle; pelican

256. Lady chapel; Assumption
258. Nave aisle; Demi-figure

WINCHESTER, NAVE AISLES

259. Adam and Eve
261. Monks and dog

260. Bagpipe player
262. Man's head

WINCHESTER, BOSSES OVER NAVE WINDOWS; GROTESQUE FIGURES

263.
265.

264.
266.

WINCHESTER, VAULTING UNDER TOWER

267. Arms of See
269. Arms of Laud

268. Charles I and his Queen
270. Arms of Bishop Curle

271. Winchester, vaulting under the tower. Compare this with 267–70 to see the difference
between ordinary vision and telephotography

WINDSOR

272. Quire; Trinity, and Bishop Fox's pelican

273. Quire; arms of Edward the Confessor

274. Quire; Tudor arms

275. Crossing; royal arms, 1528

WINDSOR, QUIRE

276. Initials H and K for Henry VIII and Katherine of Aragon

277. Badge of Thomas Howard, Earl of Surrey, later 3rd Duke of Norfolk

278. Badge of Thomas Grey, 5th Marquess of Dorset

279. Badge of William FitzAlan, 11th Earl of Arundel

WINDSOR

280. Nave; the Cross Naid   281. Edward IV and Bishop Beauchamp before the Cross
282. Roses   283. Hemp bray

WORCESTER

284. Lady chapel; Virgin and Child

285. South transept; St Dunstan

286. Nave, north aisle; Nativity

287. Nave; grotesque

WORCESTER, CLOISTERS

288. Coronation

290. Jesse

289. Bishop, with outgrowing stem

291. David

292. Amesbury; the Devil chewing Judas
294. Stoodleigh; mermaid

293. Southwark; the Devil chewing Judas
295. Stratford-sub-Castle

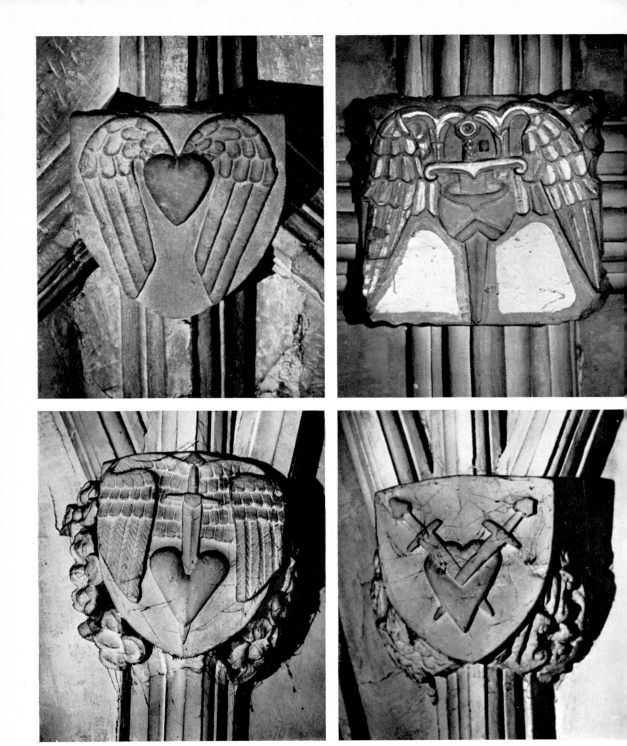

ARMA VIRGINIS

296. Hereford   297. Beverley, St Mary
298. Bristol Cathedral   299. Bristol Cathedral

FOLIATE HEADS

300. Boxgrove   301. Exeter
302. Warmington   303. Warmington

FOLIATE HEADS

304. Patrington 305. Worcester
306. Hereford 307. Hereford

FOLIATE HEADS

308. Tewkesbury	309. Ely, quire
310. Ely, Lady Chapel	311. Ely, Lady Chapel

FOLIATE HEADS

312. Norwich, cloisters
314. Winchester, nave aisle

313. Norwich, cloisters
315. Canterbury, Black Prince's chantry

FOLIATE HEADS

316. Sampford Courtenay   317. Sampford Courtenay
318. Pershore   319. Pershore

FOLIAGE; CANTERBURY, QUIRE

320. Early boss
322. Later boss

321. Early boss
323. Later boss

FOLIAGE

324. Southwark, quire, east end   325. Southwark, quire, west end
326. Blyth Priory   327. Blyth Priory

FOLIAGE; LINCOLN

328. St Hugh's quire   329. South-west transept

330. Nave   331. Angel quire

FOLIAGE

332. Chichester, retroquire   333. Chichester, Bishop's Chapel
334. Hereford, quire   335. Hereford, quire

NATURALISTIC FOLIAGE; LINCOLN, ANGEL QUIRE

336. Oak
338. Yellow water-lily

337. Hawthorn
339. Indeterminate

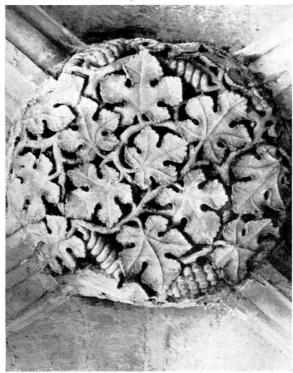

NATURALISTIC FOLIAGE; EXETER

340. Wormwood   341. Vine

342. Oak   343. Rose

FOLIAGE; ELY

344. Presbytery, Early English   345. Quire, Decorated
346. Lady Chapel   347. Lady Chapel

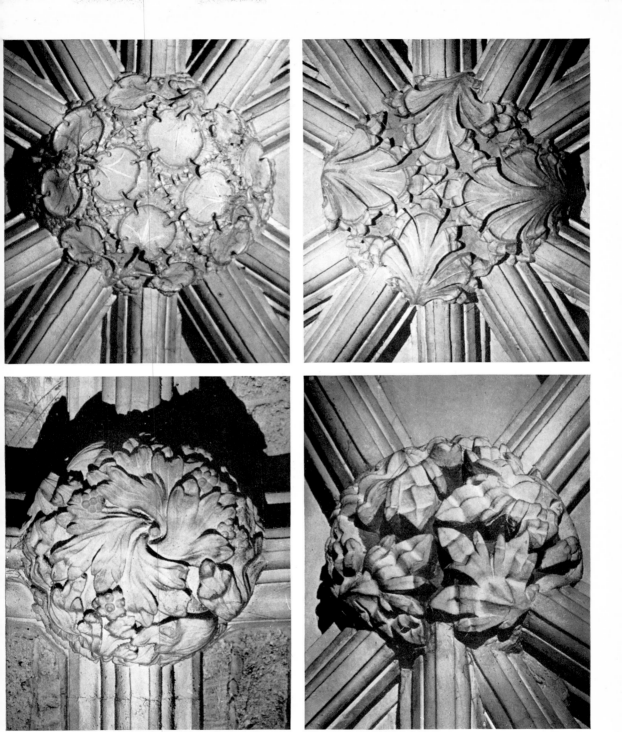

FOLIAGE, DECORATED; BRISTOL CATHEDRAL

348. Quire

350. Elder Lady Chapel

349. Quire

351. North transept

LATE NATURALISTIC FOLIAGE

352. Bristol, St Mary, Redcliffe   353. Canterbury
354. Bristol Cathedral   355. Meavy

FRENCH ROOF BOSSES

356. Troyes, St Jean
358. Rouen, St Maclou

357. Caudebec
359. Evreux

FRENCH ROOF BOSSES

360. Semur

361. Auxerre

362. Troyes Cathedral

363. Evreux

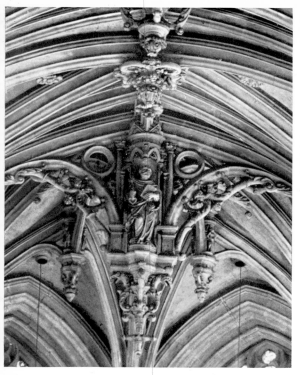

FRENCH ROOF BOSSES

364. Caen, St Pierre

365. Argentan

366. Grand Andelay

367. Pont d'Arches

THE ROYAL TECHNICAL COLLEGE
LIBRARY
GLASGOW

APPENDIX I

LIST OF CHURCHES CONTAINING ROOF BOSSES

[This list does not aim at completeness, but mention is made of cathedrals and churches in Great Britain which are known to me to have bosses of some interest or importance. Names of places which I have not visited personally are in square brackets.—C. J. P. C.]

ABBEY DORE. Some of the vaulting-ribs cross each other with no ornament; others have very small ornaments of foliage in the centre of the crossing ribs (cf. Pershore). There are also some late thirteenth- or early fourteenth-century bosses now kept in the ambulatory which came from elsewhere, perhaps from cloisters.

ABERDEEN, ST MACHAR'S CATHEDRAL. On a flat roof put up about 1520 by Bishop Dunbar is a magnificent set of forty-eight wooden heraldic bosses, colouring probably modern; the arms include those of Pope Leo X, of Edward the Confessor, the Empire, Scotland, England, and France, two archbishops and many bishops of Scottish sees, and many nobles of the kingdom of Scotland (9-12).

AMESBURY. Late bosses, perhaps early sixteenth-century, on wooden roof in nave and south transept. In nave a bishop, a cardinal, and two kings, one old and one young; a man pole-axing an ox (cf. a misericord at Worcester). In south transept the Devil chewing Judas (292); also a number of heads, male and female, some grotesque, some foliate. In nave and transept angels with shields, etc. Some have lost their wings.

ARUNDEL.[1] In the FitzAlan Chapel, on the modern roof, are wooden bosses from an older roof; fourteen demi-figures of old men, probably prophets; heads of priests and two mitred heads; a horse, the badge of FitzAlan; two angels with musical instruments—all fourteenth-century. At Poling are six

[1] C. J. P. Cave, 'The Wooden Roof Bosses in the FitzAlan Chapel, Arundel, and in Poling Church', *Sussex Archaeological Collections*, vol. LXXIII.

wooden bosses said to have come from the FitzAlan Chapel; one has four heads of children chin to chin; another four lions' heads, tongue to tongue; the others foliage (13-16).

ST AUSTELL, CORNWALL. Wagon roofs with numerous wooden bosses, all foliage save one with Passion emblems, scourges.

BANWELL, SOMERSET. Wagon roofs with over one hundred wooden bosses; an Image of Pity, a pelican, a number of heads, and eleven bosses of St George, mounted, slaying the dragon.

BEAULIEU ABBEY. Several Early English bosses in the Abbey ruins. In the refectory (now the parish church) are interesting bosses on the wagon roof; heads including a pope, kings, a Virgin queen; also an antelope, a lion, a stag and three fish *tête à la queue*. Some bosses are modern, including one of the arms of the Abbey with a date 1204.

BERE REGIS, DORSET. Hammer-beam roof erected by Cardinal Morton; a number of heads, mostly rather crude; on the hammer-beams are images of the twelve apostles.

BEVERLEY MINSTER. A few figure bosses; in the north-east transept a centaur and beasts; in the second bay of the nave a merman and mermaid; most of the nave bosses are fourteenth-century foliage. The bosses at the west end of the nave and nave aisles were made by Baker of London, *c*. 1901. In the retro-quire screen there are a few good bosses, including a Coronation (48). Besides the actual bosses there are a great number of figures and heads in the nave, and, to be specially noted, the angels with musical instruments between the arches.

BEVERLEY, ST MARY. A wealth of wooden bosses; in the whole church I estimate that there are 587. The chancel roof dates from about 1445. The bosses are well carved and of much interest; there are many heads, some must have been carved from life; there are many grotesques, such as beasts with human heads; the heads of Athelstan and St John of Beverley side by side (which also appears in the nave); the head of Christ, angels with shields; two double-headed eagles collared with a crown; and many other bosses. In the sacristy is a stone boss of a soul being carried in a napkin by two angels.

In 1520 the tower fell, wrecking part of the nave; the rebuilding took four years; the bosses and those in the north chapel are of this period. It is hardly possible to summarize them; many are grotesques; there are figures of men, women, beasts, foliate heads, etc. In the north chapel are bosses rather in the same style, including a good one of the fox preaching to the geese; a number of the bosses have lettering; there is a fine set of corbels of men playing musical instruments. In the north transept are the four symbols of the evangelists surrounded by points probably meant for rays of light (17-28, 297).

BISHOPSTONE, WILTS. Good stone bosses, including a Coronation, evangelistic symbols, and some naturalistic foliage.

BLAKENEY, NORFOLK. Two, with very good Early English foliage, in chancel; rather elaborate quatrefoils in the nave, some with faces in the middle.

BLISLAND, CORNWALL. Wagon roofs with about 190 wooden bosses; rafters, purlines, and wall-plates richly carved.

BLUNHAM, BEDS. Peculiar wooden bosses; a kneeling man, and a kneeling angel; beasts, including a chained bear (50).

BLYTH PRIORY. Three fine Early English bosses in nave; angle head with mouth foliage in style of New Shoreham; another boss with dragon, and one with foliage only (326, 327).

BLYTHBURGH, SUFFOLK. Round wooden bosses on principal rafters with conventional cloud pattern; very fine carved angels on each side, bearing coats of arms (69).

BOSTON, LINCS. Many stone bosses on vaulting under the tower; Agnus Dei in centre; also many angels. Other bosses in church modern.

BOVEY (NORTH), DEVON. Wagon roofs; in chancel very good bosses of the South Tawton type; king, queen, Virgin queen, three rabbits with but three ears between them (49), foliate heads, and several coats of arms, including a two-headed eagle, and two flying birds.

BOXGROVE PRIORY. In quire and aisles early thirteenth-century bosses, mostly conventional foliage akin to Canterbury and early Chichester bosses; one has eight heads with only eight eyes between them, alternate heads have stem from mouth (300). Late pendant bosses in La Warr chantry.

BRANCEPETH, DURHAM. In nave a number of wooden bosses; one very curious one of Christ; also a number of small bosses with Passion emblems on a supposed rood ceiling. The chancel contains unique bosses of the Laudian period with angels holding inscribed plaques (56, 57).

BRENCHLEY, KENT. A number of small wooden bosses on a rood ceiling, with angels holding scrolls or shields.

[BRIDGWATER, SOMERSET.] The chancel roof is modern, but it retains many old bosses; some very remarkable; some have inscriptions, some figure subjects. In the south transept is a roundel with a seated and crowned figure.

BRISTOL CATHEDRAL.[1] Two fine Norman bosses in the chapter-house, and other smaller ones in the entrance thereto. Interesting bosses in the north transept with arms of the Virgin, Passion emblems, various heads, and two of Edward II in his death agony. Here and under the tower good specimens of late naturalistic foliage. In the quire and sacristy are very pleasing examples of conventional Decorated foliage (7, 8, 29-32, 298, 299, 348-51).

BRISTOL, ST MARY, REDCLIFFE. Over 1100 bosses. In chancel women's heads surrounded by foliage; in south transept three heads, one in the centre of each bay, representing the Trinity; in transept aisles are Annunciation, Virgin and Child, Resurrection, and Coronation. A number of the aisle bosses have tracery like windows or vaulted roofs, and one has an actual model of the transept vaulting; also a model of a maze. The high vault of the nave has Christ seated on a rainbow, Virgin and Child, the Father holding the Crucifix, symbols of the evangelists. There are a number of bosses over the wall-plate with curious figures, one a sheila, and quite a number indecent. Under the tower are Passion emblems, a merchant's mark, various beasts, the arms of the Virgin, and a man at stool (33-43, 352).

[1] C. J. P. Cave, 'The Roof Bosses of Bristol Cathedral'. *Publication of the Friends of Bristol Cathedral*, 1935.

[BRIXHAM, DEVON.] In the south porch there is a Coronation with censing angels.

BROADCLYST, DEVON. There has been much restoration; some of the bosses are probably old, but some are certainly modern, and some are evidently modern copies of old designs, for example, the three rabbits with only three ears between them, and the sow and farrow which occur a number of times and have the appearance of modern work; a grotesque head and two dragons with necks intertwined occur rather less often, but still a number of times. There is a woman's head which is probably old, and a modern copy of it.

BROADHEMBURY, DEVON. Wagon roofs; most of the bosses are foliage, but there are three good heads and one shield with the five wounds (58, 59).

BROADWATER, SUSSEX. Three rather pleasing Early English foliage bosses are almost certainly modern.

BUCKDEN, HUNTS. A few bosses; an Assumption in the south porch; a boss with R W 1665 in chancel. A very good Agnus Dei in the Lion Hotel.

BUCKLAND MONACHORUM, DEVON. A very good set of wooden bosses of angels with musical instruments in the nave, and a Coronation.

BURWELL, CAMBS. Wooden bosses; good heads, including pope with triple crown, an emperor, a pelican, and several other birds, including a swan (46, 47).

BURY ST EDMUNDS, ST MARY. Chancel with wagon roof with 116 large and 60 smaller bosses; among the smaller are many heads, some looking like portraits, some grotesque; birds and beasts, an owl carrying a mouse in its beak. Among the larger are angels with musical instruments, with the sun and the moon; a star; various heads; a fox taking a goose, preaching to the geese, and being hanged by them; a talbot; a number of birds; a chained bear; an ape with urinary flask; a fish or dolphin; and many more. In other parts of the church a number of wooden bosses, including an archangel holding in each hand a chalice with host; the head of St Edmund being carried in a napkin by two figures, perhaps angels. In north porch a most curious boss; in centre a cusped circle with a bearded head depressed below, and partly hidden by the cusps; round this are eight arch-shaped and cusped compartments with the figure of an angel in each (52–5).

CAMBRIDGE, GREAT ST MARY. Late wooden bosses in nave; the most interesting is one of an ecclesiastic kneeling before a crucifix. There are several with angels east and west holding various objects; in one example they both hold a star; in two others one angel holds a crown the other a shield with the letter M; other bosses have St Michael slaying the Dragon, a pelican on its nest feeding its young, a plaited wreath with foliage and perhaps a fruit in the centre (51).

CANTERBURY CATHEDRAL.[1] A most important series. There is one large Norman boss in the Treasury, of four grotesque heads chin to chin. In the quire and eastern transepts a series of late twelfth-century bosses which can be accurately dated from the account of the rebuilding of the quire by Gervase. Most of them are stiff conventional foliage in the work of William of Sens, flowing trefoil foliage in that of the English William; there is a particularly fine Agnus Dei in the centre of the eastern crossing. In the crypt there are a large number of bosses possibly slightly later than those in the quire. All these bosses possibly had a great influence on the carving of roof bosses throughout the country.

In the Black Prince's chantry there are a few fourteenth-century bosses. After this there is a great series of fifteenth-century bosses in the nave, western transepts, and in the cloisters. The nave bosses are mostly small heads, some grotesque, a few armorial and a few late naturalistic foliage. In the north transept are a number of heraldic bosses of the time of Edward IV; they have been repainted in the nineteenth century. In the south walk of the cloisters there are numerous figure bosses, and in the other walks a vast series of heraldic bosses[2] (5, 60-8, 315, 320-3).

CARLISLE CATHEDRAL. The bosses in the quire are probably modern, though it is just possible that a few of them may be old ones that have been reset in the later wooden roof. Under the quire screen are a few small medieval bosses, including some quite good heads.

[1] C. J. P. Cave, 'The Roof Bosses of the Cathedral Church of Christ, Canterbury'. *The Friends of Canterbury Cathedral*, 1934.

[2] Commander A. W. B. Messenger, F.S.A., *The Heraldry of Canterbury Cathedral. The Great Cloister Vault.*

CARLISLE DEANERY. A few interesting bosses, including St Barbara, a mermaid, and a pelican.

CAWSTON, NORFOLK. Nave with hammer-beam roof with many small wooden bosses; some very good, probably late fourteenth-century. In the south transept mostly heads, also very good.

CHAGFORD, DEVON. Two bosses with three rabbits with only three ears between them, one much restored; four human heads on one boss, chin to chin, and close by a modern copy; a two-headed eagle; several heads.

CHARTHAM, KENT. One wooden boss where two beams cross at the centre of the church; this has naturalistic oak leaves with a flower rather like a periwinkle in the centre; it is extremely like some of the bosses in the Angel quire at Lincoln, so much so that it would seem to be of the same date.

CHERITON BISHOP, DEVON. Mostly foliage, but one boss with three rabbits with only three ears between them.

CHESTER CATHEDRAL. The best bosses are in the Early English Lady Chapel; the Trinity, Virgin and Child (71, 72), and the murder of St Thomas of Canterbury. There are later bosses in the north transept and in the cloisters, including two of the arms of Cardinal Wolsey. There are also some on the abbey gateway, including one of St Werburga.

CHICHESTER CATHEDRAL.[1] Interesting early foliage bosses showing marked affinity to Canterbury. Some of the aisle bosses are very like bosses at Boxgrove; there is one showing six heads with six eyes between them, each face having mouth foliage. In the quire is a late boss of an angel bearing a shield with the arms of St Richard of Chichester. There are several later bosses in various parts of the Cathedral and some good modern ones round the crossing, dating from the rebuilding after the fall of the spire (332).

CHICHESTER, CHAPEL IN BISHOP'S PALACE. Two extremely fine examples of thirteenth-century trefoil foliage (333).

---

[1] C. J. P. Cave, 'The Roof Bosses in Chichester Cathedral', *Sussex Archaeological Collections*, vol. LXXI.

CHRISTCHURCH, HANTS. Some late fifteenth- or early sixteenth-century bosses in quire; some with initials in centre. An angel carrying a church with transepts and tower. In the Salisbury chantry is a Coronation of the Virgin, much mutilated. Very fine corbels of angels holding shields with Passion emblems; also some old men.

CHUMLEIGH, DEVON. Wagon roofs with some fine heads.

[CILCEN, DENBIGH.] Hammer-beam roof with bosses in the middle of each rafter; one of a naked woman with arms crossed in front; she is apparently meant to be in a shroud which is open in front. There is also one bearded head, and some fine beasts.

CLEEVE ABBEY, SOMERSET. Wagon roof in refectory with some very fine foliage bosses.

OLD CLEEVE, SOMERSET. Wagon roof with many bosses, mostly foliage, but some beasts.

CLEY-NEXT-THE-SEA, NORFOLK. Bosses in south porch: a fox carrying off a goose and an old woman attacking it with a distaff; the Assumption; a boy birched by two apes; an owl with a mouse in its beak; some angels.

ST COLUMB MAJOR, CORNWALL. Most of the bosses are modern, but there are a few old ones; there are some modern Passion emblems in the St Neots style.

CONGRESBURY, SOMERSET. Wagon roof with very unusual wooden bosses, with foliage and geometrical designs, and some with heads in the centre (73-6).

COXWOLD, YORKS. Wooden bosses, heads, beasts, a bird and a fish or dolphin; they have been repainted, but are probably old. In the porch is an old man carrying a sack.

CRANBURY PARK, HANTS. A tower built in the eighteenth century has a number of bosses built into the walls; they came from Netley Abbey; they are very badly weathered and most of them are difficult to decipher.

CRONDALL, HANTS. Two early bosses in the chancel, probably late twelfth century, one has the Agnus Dei, the other foliage; they both show a marked affinity to Canterbury (70).

CROSCOMBE, SOMERSET. Some very fine wooden bosses; Christ in Glory, a kneeling man and a kneeling woman, a bat, a mermaid, grotesque heads, two musicians, and a phallic figure (77-80).

ST DAVID'S CATHEDRAL. Magnificent wooden pendant bosses in the nave. There are a number of other bosses in various parts of the Cathedral, some armorial. In the vestry is a Last Judgement.

ST DECUMAN'S, SOMERSET. Wagon roof with 184 wooden bosses and twenty-three half bosses; well carved, mostly with foliage, but there are a number of beasts in the Somerset style. There are also a number of angels at the feet of the braces, some having shields with Passion emblems.

DENTON, NORFOLK. Very good bosses in the north porch; in the centre is an extremely good Coronation; others are the Annunciation, the Resurrection, the Ascension, and one with two seated figures, a man and a woman, and two beasts below, one a muzzled bear. There are also several angels.

DRYBURGH ABBEY. A rather good boss of the Agnus Dei surrounded by foliage, vine leaves, and bearing the letters I H S; this is now kept in the chapter house. A few bosses still *in situ*, including one of an old man in a roundel. There are some unimportant bosses among the fragments of sculpture in one of the buildings of the cloister.

DUNSTER, SOMERSET. In chancel mostly foliage, but a boss of two dragons with intertwined necks. Nave, mostly foliage and roses, but there are some heads in the local Somerset style, like those at Luccomb but unpainted and rather worn. There are a number of shields within quatrefoils.

DURHAM CATHEDRAL.[1] There are no bosses in the nave or transepts. In the quire are three bosses with Early English trefoil foliage, some with figures also,

[1] C. J. P. Cave, 'The roof-sculptures of Durham Cathedral', *Archaeologia Aeliana* (4th ser.), vol. XIV, p. 67.

which are very difficult to make out without photographs; there are also two plaque bosses, one of the souls of the just in Abraham's bosom, the other of the Agnus Dei; both are very French in style. In the chapel of the Nine Altars are three well-holes with extremely fine carving round them; round one are the four evangelists. There is another well-hole under the central tower with a border of foliage; on the vaulting round are small fifteenth-century foliage bosses (81-4).

EDINBURGH, ST GILES. A large number of bosses, but no photographic survey has been made, and details are difficult to see owing to want of light. In the Albany aisle there is a well-hole with an ornamented border. At the west end of the north aisle of the nave is a plaque in the French style with the letter M.

EGLOSHAYLE, CORNWALL. Wooden bosses in the south aisle; they are curious in that two Passion emblems, namely the Five Wounds and the Crown of Thorns surrounding the Nails, are each repeated five times; all the rest of the bosses are foliage.

ELGIN CATHEDRAL. There are a number of bosses in the chapter-house, including Christ in Glory, a bishop, and a number of heads, some single, some in pairs, and some in groups of four; there are also some shields with arms, and one with Passion emblems.

ELKSTONE, GLOS. A single Norman boss in the chancel on which are four heads and strap work (3).

ELY CATHEDRAL.[1] In the presbytery are very fine thirteenth-century trefoil bosses (344); there are only three figure-bosses, a Coronation, St Etheldreda, and a figure holding a church and keys (85-7). In the quire are typical fourteenth-century foliage bosses (345) and four foliate heads (309). In the octagon under the apex of the arches are the four evangelists; higher up, just under the spring

[1] C. J. P. Cave, 'The Roof Bosses in Ely Cathedral', *Cambridge Antiquarian Society's Communications*, vol. XXXII, p. 33; 'A Note on some further roof bosses in Ely Cathedral', *Camb. Ant. Soc. Proc.*, vol. XXXVII, p. 50; 'The Roof Bosses in Ely Cathedral', reprinted from the *Second Annual Report of the Friends of Ely Cathedral*.

of the lantern, are eight crowned figures, six male, two female, with the lower part of their bodies wholly or partially concealed by foliage (compare the two figures at the west end of the nave at Tewkesbury). Under the summet of the lantern is a large figure of Christ surrounded by clouds, blessing and showing the wound in his side (88). In the north transept there is a series of large foliage bosses with radiating foliage of fifteenth-century type, but they have in their centres small figures, grotesque heads, a pelican and a chained bear. There are no bosses in the nave.

In the Lady Chapel there are a great number of bosses, including a head of Christ, Madonna and Child, Assumption, Coronation, Ascension, Annunciation, Visitation, and Crucifixion, in this order from the east end (89, 90, 91). There are very many heads (93-6), some of them foliate (310-11). At the west end is the translation of St Etheldreda, showing the marble coffin described by Bede (92).

EVESHAM,[1] ALL SAINTS. In the porch is an unusual Passion emblem representation.[2] In the sixteenth-century chapel is a good pendant boss with the initials C P L for Clement Lichfield, prior and later abbot of Evesham. On the floor of this chapel are kept three bosses which are said to have come from the Abbey, a pelican feeding its young, a bearded head with long hair, and an angel holding a shield bearing the arms of the abbey.

EVESHAM, ST LAURENCE.[1] In the chapel built by Abbot Lichfield is a good pendant boss.

EXETER CATHEDRAL.[3] One of the finest collections of roof bosses in the country, dating from the end of the thirteenth century at the east end to the end of the fourteenth century at the west end. There is no series as at Norwich or Tewkesbury, the subjects being arranged in a rather haphazard manner. Among the subjects are five Crucifixions, two Coronations, Christ in Glory, Samson and the lion three times, St John the Baptist with the Agnus Dei, the crucifixion of St Andrew, and many other figures. There are also many beasts, birds, dragons, a mermaid (twice), a centaur. In the ambulatory are some extremely

[1] 'The Bosses in the sixteenth-century chapels in All Saints and St Laurence Churches, Evesham', *Transactions of the Worcestershire Archaeological Society*, vol. XVIII (New Series), p. 47.

[2] 'All Saints Church, Evesham: the Wooden Boss in the Porch', *Trans. Worc. Arch. Soc.*, vol. XVI (New Series), p. 57.

[3] E. K. Prideaux and G. R. Holt Shafto, *Bosses and Corbels of Exeter Cathedral*.

good examples of naturalistic foliage, some with beasts and birds among the foliage. There is an immense number of heads, one possibly intended for Isabella wife of Edward II, and one for Philippa wife of Edward III; the head of a pope must be meant for John XXII. In the nave is one of the finest bosses in the country representing the murder of St Thomas of Canterbury, dating from about the middle of the fourteenth century; there is a full-length figure of Bishop Grandison, possibly intended as a portrait, and a kneeling figure of Canon William de Weston the bishop's right-hand man. Including foliage there are over 370 bosses in the Cathedral. There is also an unrivalled collection of corbels.

The quire bosses are interesting because they show two different styles; there is a change of style at the fifth bay; the foliage from being naturalistic becomes conventional with knobs and bulges on the leaves; the heads too in the western bays lack the grace of the earlier ones. The change is quite abrupt. The first four bays of the quire, strictly the presbytery, were finished by 1307, the year of Bishop Bytton's death; the four western ones were finished by his successor. Prebendary H. E. Bishop[1] assumes that these bosses were carved in the work-shop in Bytton's time, as payments for them occur in the fabric rolls for 1303; but though they may have been got ready at this early date it is probable that the final carvings were not done till later, for it is most probable that the carving of roof bosses was done *in situ* after the boss was in position (see Chapter 1, p. 2) (97-104).

[FORTROSE CATHEDRAL.] In the south aisle there is some original vaulting with bosses bearing the arms of Leslie and Bullock, showing that the roof was built by Alexander, Earl of Ross, during the episcopate of Bishop Bullock (1420–39).[2]

FOWEY, CORNWALL. Wagon roof with 157 bosses; all are foliage except two, each of which has a Passion emblem of a heart surrounded by the Crown of Thorns.

FURNEAUX PELHAM, HERTS. Bosses with leopards' heads and roses; in the nave are angels on the wall-plate; two with shields of arms, two with musical instruments; in the south aisle of the chancel is an angel holding the Crown of Thorns.

[1] *The Building of the Cathedral Church of St Peter in Exeter*, p. 47.
[2] Ian Gordon Lindsay, *The Cathedrals of Scotland*, p. 135.

GEDNEY, LINCS. A number of bosses rather in the style of those in the nave of Salle. They are mostly foliage, though there are a number of heads, some with mouth foliage; there are one or two angels with shields, a head of Christ, and several Passion emblems. Some of the foliage bosses have heads in their centres.

GLASGOW CATHEDRAL. A large number of bosses in the two crypts; there are many heads, some in groups of four; there are several dragons with foliage; two examples of the Agnus Dei; a skull surrounded by leaves with worms above the eye-sockets; there are a number of shields of arms, some with supporters or held by angels, one has the royal arms of Scotland. The bosses are not in very good condition; they seem to be fifteenth century.

GLOUCESTER CATHEDRAL.[1] The seven eastern bays of the nave have very fine mid-thirteenth century bosses with trefoil foliage, and some with dragons; there are small bosses of the same date in the 'Reliquary' in the north transept. In the quire, mid-fourteenth century, is a figure of Christ surrounded by angels bearing musical instruments, two with Passion emblems, and one holding a palm (105-12). The north transept has a number of slightly later bosses, mostly foliage, but a few with beasts and two with foliate heads. There are no carved bosses in the south transept. In the two western bays of the nave and in the south porch are early fifteenth-century bosses, the most outstanding one being a Coronation. In the centre of the porch is a plaque boss with a demi-figure of Christ showing the stigmata; surrounding it are a number of figures of angels. In the Lady Chapel, latter half of the fifteenth century, are a large number of bosses, mostly foliage, but some with very curious beasts and fishes; these bosses are very peculiar and unlike any I know of elsewhere.

GODALMING, SURREY. An interesting series of heraldic bosses, including the arms of Richard Fox, bishop of Winchester, the Howard arms without the Flodden augmentation, and many others; also the Prince of Wales's feathers. In 1500 Fox became Bishop of Winchester, in which diocese Godalming then was, and after Henry VIII came to the throne in 1509 there was no Prince of Wales for 101 years; the bosses presumably date from between 1500 and 1509.

[1] C. J. P. Cave, 'The Roof Bosses in Gloucester Cathedral', *Transactions of the Bristol and Gloucestershire Archaeological Society*, vol. 53, p. 99.

[HARTLAND, DEVON.] Wagon roofs with a number of bosses, but those in the north aisle are modern.

HASLINGFIELD, CAMBS. Some very good wooden bosses with trefoil foliage in the aisles; there are some later bosses loose in the church.

[HASTINGS, ALL SAINTS, SUSSEX.] A well-hole under the tower with signs of the Zodiac round it.

HATHERLEIGH, DEVON. Wagon roofs with bosses, all foliage except two at the east end of the south aisle; one has four heads, the other the head of a woman in pedimental head-dress. There is a rood ceiling in the nave with ornamented panels; on the wall-plates there are a number of angels with plain shields.

HAVANT, HANTS. Two early thirteenth-century bosses in the chancel with affinities to those at Chichester and Boxgrove.

HAVERFORDWEST, PEMB. Many wooden bosses, most of them foliage, but there are a few heads amidst the foliage; some of the nave bosses are short pendants; a boss at the west end of the nave has four angle heads, one of them with mouth foliage.

[HAYES, MIDDLESEX.] Wooden roof with small bosses.

[HEMSBY, NORFOLK.] A fine set of bosses in the porch with scenes from the life of Our Lady, including the Nativity. There are also bosses in the nave.

HEREFORD CATHEDRAL. The quire bosses have good trefoil foliage, two with flowers in the centre, one meant for a rose, the other like a periwinkle. The Lady Chapel, besides foliage bosses, has an extremely curious boss of a head (of Christ?) with two dragons below, one with mouth foliage.

In the Audley chantry is a late but good Assumption. In the south transept are the arms of Our Lady, a heart flanked by wings (296), and also a coat of two crosiers in saltire, a mitre-in-chief.

In the nave aisles are a number of heads closely surrounded by leaves, some with mouth foliage (306, 307). In the south aisle is a head with closed eyes and a protruding tongue; there is also a seated figure of Christ in a vesica piscis. In the cloisters is a heart with a small trefoil on the top, the whole surrounded by a scroll with inscription.

In the nave are a number of wooden foliage bosses of the time of Wyatt.

HEXHAM ABBEY. In the quire aisles are simple foliage and petal bosses rather in the style of Chichester. The high roof of the transept is wooden with some good fifteenth-century bosses, one the head of Christ. The eastern aisles of the transepts are stone vaulted; in the north transept aisles are flat plaques with foliage.

IFFLEY, OXON. One Norman boss in chancel with coiled dragons (2).

ST JUST-IN-ROSELAND, CORNWALL. A number of flat painted bosses in the chancel; the central line has geometrical designs, the side lines have Passion emblems. The paintings are worn, and some rather crude; it is just possible that the work is nineteenth-century or touched up then, but local evidence is against this. Professor Tristram, from an examination of the photographs, thinks the work is medieval but very late. Among the subjects are an Agnus Dei, an emblem of the Trinity, the letter M crowned, a seven-branched candlestick, a phœnix, ⚶ with A and Ω on each side, three fish with the word ΙΧΘΥΣ above, and the following Passion emblems: a lantern with staves crossed behind it and a sword on either side, a spear and a sponge on a reed in saltire with a label in front with the letters INRI and a crown above, another with a ladder behind and a nail on either side, hammer and pincers, three nails and the Crown of Thorns, a pillar with a cock on it and a scourge and birch-rod on either side, the seamless coat and three dice. These are the only uncarved painted bosses I know; they are the only ones with any Greek lettering, with the exception of one which is almost certainly modern; my impression is that they are very late medieval work (113-114).

ST KEW, CORNWALL. The wagon roofs in this church are typical of so many Cornish examples; there are a large number of bosses, forty-five in the chancel, seventy in the nave, thirty-six in the north aisle, and forty-two in the south aisle, 193 in all; they are all foliage or conventional floral designs, and, as so often is the case in Cornwall, the same design is often repeated on all the bosses on the same rafter.

KILKHAMPTON, CORNWALL. Some rather good wooden bosses; the Crown of Thorns surrounding three nails is repeated three times on the same rafter; one boss has the arms of three clarions for Granville. There are a few modern bosses.

KILPECK, HEREFORD. One Norman boss in the chancel with four beaked heads (4).

KING'S LYNN, ST NICHOLAS. In the porch God the Father in triple crown, eight angels in surrounding bosses, and other bosses with a queen, a bishop, etc.

KING'S NYMPTON, DEVON. Some very remarkable wooden foliate heads, also some Passion emblems. As in a number of late wagon roofs, the same design is repeated several times on the same rafter. The porch has a most unusual wagon roof with forty or fifty bosses, almost all foliage; there is one knot (115, 116).

[KIRKSTEAD, LINCS, ST LEONARD'S CHAPEL.] Early English vaulting with a boss in each of four bays, one boss being an Agnus Dei surrounded by trefoil foliage.

LACOCK ABBEY, WILTS. The cloisters have a very large collection of fifteenth-century bosses, including Agnus Dei, pelican, mermaid, jester, acrobats, birds, beasts, etc., an angel with a sword in one hand and a viol in the other; there are also a number of heads, some of them foliate. A very interesting set.

LACOCK, WILTS. In the Lady Chapel of the parish Church are a number of bosses probably carved by the craftsmen who carved those in the abbey cloisters; there are angels bearing shields with Passion emblems, and two with chalice and host; some beasts, one a fox carrying off a goose.

LAMBETH PALACE. Wooden bosses in the Post Room, mostly of angels carrying shield, book, scroll, etc.

LANLIVERY, CORNWALL. Richly carved purlines, rafters, and wall-plates, with good bosses, mostly foliage of the Cornish type; there are three or four heads, mostly grotesque.

LANREATH, CORNWALL. Curious square wooden bosses with an inner square enclosing some design.

LANSALLOS, CORNWALL. Some rather good wooden bosses, mostly foliage of the Cornish type, but one plain cross. The bosses in the chancel are modern.

LAUNCESTON, CORNWALL. Wagon roofs with 375 bosses and 30 half-bosses; all foliage with two or three possible exceptions. The carving seems poor.

LECHLADE, GLOS.[1] A number of wooden angels with Passion emblems not treated armorially. Other angels carry shields with no arms; one carries a scroll, possibly the label of the Crucifixion. There is an interesting boss of two men wrestling.

The bosses were taken down owing to repairs to the roof; they were to be repainted when I saw them in 1938; the work was completed in 1939. A curious point came to light, namely that the bosses were made for some other roof, as the manner in which they are cut away at the back does not fit the present roof.

LEICESTER, ST MARY. Roof restored in 1934 owing to death-watch beetle, but old timbers and bosses were replaced; there are some curious angels and some heads, including grotesques.

LICHFIELD CATHEDRAL. A good series of bosses, mostly fourteenth century. In the quire a Last Judgement, a Trinity, with the Father holding the Crucifix, a Coronation with an angel above who would have been holding the crown, but the heads of all three figures have been broken and have been replaced with what look like lumps of clay; there is also an Assumption. In the north quire aisle is another Coronation, also an angel holding a shield bearing the arms of the see. In the south quire aisle is an Annunciation and a head closely surrounded by leaves which is very similar to heads at Hereford. There are some early bosses in the east aisles of the transepts, one has an eagle tearing at the neck of a lamb which carries something on its back.

At the east end of the nave is a Visitation, but it looks of rather doubtful antiquity. In the north aisle in the seventh bay from the east is a boss with very

[1] C. J. P. Cave, 'Roof Bosses at Lechlade', *Transactions of the Bristol and Gloucestershire Archaeological Society*, vol. 60, p. 47, 1939.

early trefoil foliage; it looks earlier than its surroundings and may have been made for some other position, and, being left over, was made use of here.[1] In the south aisle is Samson and the Lion. In the chapter-house are some thirteenth-century foliage bosses, and a good lion amid foliage. In the chapter-house entrance is a coiled dragon with mouth foliage (117-20).

LINCOLN CATHEDRAL.[2] A series of bosses showing the evolution of trefoil foliage from St Hugh's quire at the end of the twelfth century through the freer foliage of the early thirteenth century to the splendid trefoil and naturalistic foliage in the Angel quire of the second part of the thirteenth century. There are not many figure bosses except in the aisles of the Angel quire where there are extremely fine ones; these include a Coronation, a king and prophet, an apostle and prophet, a Tree of Jesse, a woman and two pet dogs, wrestlers, a naked man fighting with a merman, a man and woman kissing across a vaulting-rib, dragons, and others.

In most of the Cathedral, but not in the Angel quire, there is not a proper fit between the vaulting-ribs and the keystone, and therefore it is probable that these bosses were made in the workshop and not carved after the boss was *in situ*.

The roof of the cloisters is very remarkable, for though of wood, dating from the last years of the thirteenth century, it is made in imitation of stone vaulting, as also at Warmington. The bosses are very much weathered, but even in their present state some of them are very fine. Some appear to be occupations of the months and there may have been more in the now destroyed north walk.

In the Galilee porch there is one boss which is different from its neighbours, and is in the style of those in St Hugh's quire for which it was probably made, and being left over was used here; the joining up with the vaulting-ribs is extremely clumsy (121-33, 328-31).

LIFTON, DEVON. Wagon roof with wooden bosses; two pelicans, one in nave, one in chancel, and a double-headed eagle; these bosses are just like some at Morwenstowe and must have been carved by the same craftsmen; there are also several heads.

[1] Compare a boss in the Galilee porch at Lincoln.
[2] Papers on the bosses of the east walk of the cloisters by Rev. E. Venables, *Associated Architectural Societies' Reports and Papers*, vol. XX, p. 179; *Archaeological Journal*, vol. XLVII, p. 220; and *The Builder*, vol. LIX, p. 48; C. J. P. Cave, 'The Roof Bosses of Lincoln Cathedral', *Archaeologia*, vol. LXXXV, p. 23.

LONDON, ST ANDREW UNDERSHAFT. A number of small early sixteenth-century wooden bosses, including an Agnus Dei, also some pomegranates, and one combined with a rose, showing that the date must be prior to 1529.

LONDON, ST BARTHOLOMEW THE GREAT. A few old bosses are incorporated into the rebuilt cloister vaulting; they are mostly foliage, but there is one head. There are a number of bosses which have not been re-erected, including a head of Christ, an Annunciation, the figure of the Virgin having been broken away, a mermaid, and a bird, perhaps a pelican.

LONG SUTTON, SOMERSET. A very rich low-pitched king-post roof in the nave, with large foliage bosses. The bosses in the chancel are modern.

LOUTH, LINCS. On the wall inside the north door are placed three small wooden bosses, one of Christ in Glory. Large wooden foliage bosses in the nave. Under the tower is stone-vaulting with bosses.

LUCCOMBE, SOMERSET. Some good heads of the local Somerset type; several bosses in the nave have leaves something like beech.

LUDLOW, SALOP. Interesting bosses in the chancel, probably late fifteenth or early sixteenth century; angels, beasts' heads, two women, a bishop, an old man, a bird with a woman's head, a falcon on a fetterlock, etc. There has been modern repainting, including some modern lettering.

LUTTERWORTH, LEICESTER. A large number of angels, mostly carrying shields, and a few other bosses.

ST MADRON, CORNWALL. A number of grotesque heads, nearly all with protruding tongues; two double-headed eagles; a fish.

MALMESBURY ABBEY. Many very fine foliage bosses, and a few heads. In the north aisle are several fragments of bosses, including one of the Assumption and one with Passion emblems.

[MANCHESTER CATHEDRAL.] Many wooden bosses, including a very interesting set of angels bearing musical instruments.

MARKET HARBOROUGH, LEICESTER. A number of wooden angels and some rather good heads; the latter may, however, be modern. The bosses in the nave aisles are all modern.

MATTINGLEY, HANTS. A small wooden Agnus Dei.

MEAVY, DEVON. Wagon roof with a large number of wooden bosses of an unusual style; grotesque heads, one with a mouse in one ear and the mouse's tail showing in the other; a head of Christ; some foliage bosses, and several examples of very late but quite good naturalistic foliage (134-7, 355).

MELROSE ABBEY. In the quire are a number of bosses, mostly poor and much weathered; in the centre is a Trinity with the Father holding the Crucifix.

MILDENHALL, SUFFOLK. Like so many East Anglian churches the only bosses are in the porch. Here there are seventeen, but all are badly worn.

MILFORD-ON-SEA, HANTS. Wooden bosses; a number of heads, some foliate; possibly very late.

MILTON ABBOT, DEVON. Wagon roofs; bosses mostly foliage, but two unusual examples of Madonna and Child, head and shoulders only; several other heads, including one 'toothache'. Some of the foliage bosses are very good.

MORWENSTOWE, CORNWALL. A few bosses, including a pelican and a double-headed eagle exactly like examples at Lifton. A boss over the rood of an angel with upraised hands and a shield in front was found recently and placed in its present position.

NANTWICH, CHESHIRE. The lierne vault in the chancel of this perpendicular church has a number of very good bosses; the central ones from east to west are Christ in Glory, Coronation, Annunciation, Assumption, Annunciation (again), St Anne and the Virgin, Nativity, Scourging, Crucifixion, Resurrection, 'Noli me tangere'; there are also various heads, foliage, etc.

ST NEOT, CORNWALL. The chancel bosses with Passion emblems are all modern, and bosses of the same type are found elsewhere in Cornwall, and also under the organ loft at St Pancras Old Church, London. In the north aisles are wooden bosses of the usual Cornish type, all five bosses on the same rafter being alike. The nave bosses are peculiar, rather like those at Lanreath, with cusped borders enclosing letters or numbers; the half-boss at the west end has the date 1593, but the actual bosses may be earlier.

NEWBURY, BERKS. The present church was built by John Winchcombe or Smalwode ('Jack of Newbury'), but was probably not finished till after his death. A corbel gives a date 1532, probably the date of completion. There are a number of wooden bosses and a series of angels carrying shields with Passion emblems. All these have been repainted and many probably restored when the roof has been repaired or renewed at various dates. The bosses and angels in the chancel seem to be modern. The initials I W and I S occur on bosses. There are also arms which appear to be those of the sees of Winchester, Exeter, and Gloucester.

NEWCASTLE-UPON-TYNE CATHEDRAL. A large number of late wooden bosses, mostly heraldic with a border of foliage; some shields are carried by an angel. There is a mermaid in the north transept and a lion's head foliate.

NORWICH CATHEDRAL.[1] There are more bosses here than in any other cathedral in England. The earliest are those in the cloisters, dating from the end of the thirteenth century to about 1430. There are over 300 figure bosses here, with a very great variety of subjects, the most interesting being those illustrating the Apocalypse which are found in the south and west walks; but there are very many other subjects of great interest. In the Bauchon chantry there are some forty-seven bosses dating from about 1450, including an Assumption and a Coronation, together with some angels; the rest of the bosses consist of a medieval story which in the main is that of Chaucer's *Man of Law's Tale*.

[1] Dr M. R. James, 'The Sculptured Bosses in the roof of the Bauchon Chapel', *Norfolk and Norwich Archaeological Society*, 1908; 'The Sculptured Bosses in the Cloisters of Norwich Cathedral', *Norfolk and Norwich Archaeological Society*, 1911. *The Thirteen Hundredth Anniversary of the Diocese of East Anglia*, *Official Handbook*, p. 55, 1930.

C. J. P. Cave, 'The Roof Bosses in the Transepts of Norwich Cathedral Church', *Archaeologia*, vol. LXXXIII, p. 45, 1933.

Prof. E. W. Tristram, 'The Cloister Bosses, Norwich Cathedral', reprinted from the *Sixth, Seventh,* and *Eighth Annual Reports of the Friends of the Cathedral Church of Norwich*, 1938.

Dean Goulburn and the Rev. H. Symonds, *The Ancient Sculptures in the Roof of Norwich Cathedral*, 1876. Only the nave bosses are dealt with.

The nave has 255 bosses with subjects from the Old and the New Testaments, from the Creation to the Last Judgement, and ending with a boss of Bishop Lyhart (1446–72) who gave the nave roof.

The quire was vaulted under Bishop Goldwell (1472–99); there are a very few figure bosses here, but there is a Trinity and an Assumption; there are also a large number of bosses with the Bishop's rebus, a gold well, which in some cases is held by an angel.

The transept bosses were made when the roof was rebuilt under Bishop Nykke (1501–36) after a fire in 1509. There are 150 bosses mostly representing scenes from the early life of Christ. They are exceptionally small in size, the largest being only about 1 ft. 8 in. in diameter, and some only about 8 in. They contain many unusual subjects: the life and death of St John the Baptist, scenes in which Herod occurs, including his death; the childhood of Christ, the Nativity, the Shepherds, the Magi, the Circumcision, the Flight into Egypt; also the Calling of the Apostles, the Temptation, Christ asleep in the ship, preaching from a ship, healing the sick, casting out devils, the Marriage Feast at Cana, and very many more scenes (138-65, 312, 313).

NORWICH, ST HELEN'S HOSPITAL. In the south transept is an extremely interesting series; in the centre is a Coronation, the figures of Christ and the Virgin being surrounded by angels; on bosses surrounding this are the Annunciation, Nativity, Resurrection, Ascension, the Apostles, and many other figures.

In the chancel, now part of the hospital, is a wagon roof with very many bosses, mostly foliage, but nine of them bear human heads and three lions' heads (166-9).

NORWICH, ST PETER MANCROFT. Numerous wooden bosses, including an Agnus Dei.

OCKHAM,[1] SURREY. Some curious wooden bosses, including a hemp bray, a fish-trap, a grotesque head, etc.

ORWELL, CAMBS. In the Perpendicular chancel along the central rib are four three-quarter length figures; each has the left arm flexed over the lower part of the body; two have the right arm raised, and two have it flexed over the breast. I have come across no figures like them elsewhere; it is difficult to know

---

[1] Richard Bloxam, 'The Nave Roof of Ockham Church, Surrey', *The Builder*, 6 August (1937), p. 226.

whether they are meant to be men or women, but I have a suspicion that they may be phallic. Figures on the sides of the roof are heads of bearded men or of beasts, the latter with protruding tongues.

OTTERY ST MARY, DEVON. Some extremely good bosses dating from about the middle of the fourteenth century, including the Virgin and Child (twice) the Annunciation, the Coronation, St Anne and the Virgin, St John the Baptist, and Bishop Grandison (170-3).

OUNDLE, NORTHANTS. Nave and chancel have a number of small wooden heads carved on the lower part of the collar braces, a very unusual arrangement; some of these are very good. In the south aisle are some grotesque heads. On the main panels of the stone vaulting under the tower are three small heads, and a square block evidently meant to be carved but left unfinished. In the porch are some stone bosses, an angel with a shield and some good late naturalistic foliage.

OVERBURY, GLOS. Two bosses, a queen and a fish with a human head.

OXFORD, CHRIST CHURCH. In the north aisle of the quire there are four leaves on the intersection of Norman vaulting-ribs, but it is a matter of doubt if this is a Norman carving.

In the chapter-house are four extremely good thirteenth-century bosses, Christ in Glory, the Virgin and Child, St Frideswide, and four lion's bodies joined to one head.

In the cathedral there are some good fourteenth-century bosses in the Latin Chapel, including some naturalistic foliage, a king's head and a squirrel.

The elaborate late fifteenth-century vaulting of the quire has a great many bosses, not however of very high merit; they include a head of Christ, an archbishop, a bishop with two attendants, a woman crowned with a sceptre in one hand and a book (?) in the other, with an angel on either side, a Virgin and Child, and a great many heads, some with mouth foliage, and one of a bishop putting on his mitre.

OXFORD, DIVINITY SCHOOL. The late Sir William St John Hope has given a full account of this outstanding fifteenth-century roof and of its 455 bosses.[1]

[1] 'The Heraldry and Sculptures of the Vault of the Divinity School at Oxford', *Archaeological Journal*, vol. LXXI, no. 283; 2nd Series, vol. XXI, no. 3, pp. 217–60.

Many of these are heraldic, and 'many are carved with words or monograms in black letter; it would, in fact, be difficult to think of another vault which displays so much lettering as this does'.

There are besides four figure bosses: 1. Veronica with her kerchief, the whole surrounded by the Crown of Thorns. 2. The Trinity represented by two demi-figures, the Father crowned and holding a globe in one hand and blessing with the other, the Son crowned with the Crown of Thorns and showing the stigmata; standing on their shoulders is the Dove with wings outspread behind the heads of the other two figures. 3. The Virgin and Child; the former being a demi-figure, crowned, and holding the Child who has an orb in his left hand, and with his right is holding his left foot; the figures have rays round them and a thin crescent below. 4. The Agnus Dei, an unusual representation, the Lamb being couchant on a book with the cross and banner behind; the Crown of Thorns surrounds the whole.

OXFORD, MERTON COLLEGE. Under the FitzJames gateway (c. 1500, restored 1905) are the Signs of the Zodiac with the royal arms and supporters in the centre; some of these are fine and very natural, but some are very quaint, especially the scorpion which is completely unlike the real scorpion[1] (174-7).

OXFORD, ST PETER IN THE EAST. In the chancel are very small carvings at the intersection of the vaulting-ribs in the two bays; in one of the bays the ribs are carved like chains, presumably to represent St Peter's chains.

PATRINGTON, YORKS. In the east aisle of the south transept, besides many curious foliate heads (304), there is a very unusual pendant boss with a rose below, and three niches on the sides with figures of the Annunciation, St John the Baptist, and St Katherine. It is somewhat reminiscent of French pendants.

PAYHEMBURY, DEVON. Wagon roofs, but almost all the bosses are modern; there are Passion emblems in the chancel exactly in the style of those at St Columb Major, and St Neot, Cornwall and in St Pancras Old Church, London.

---

[1] See *Royal Commission on Historical Monuments: City of Oxford*, p. 77 b and Plate 139, where illustrations are given of the royal arms and of Taurus, Gemini, Scorpio, Leo, Virgo, Sagittarius, Aquarius, and Pisces; but Scorpio is wrongly attributed to Cancer; the latter, which is not illustrated, is a very good representation of a crab.

PERSHORE ABBEY. In the quire aisles are some early small roundels on the intersection of the vaulting-ribs, with a small star in the centre of each. The high vault of the quire has some very beautiful naturalistic foliage, and some foliate heads. The south transept has some later bosses, including some foliate heads, one of a king, and some coats of arms (318, 319).

PETERBOROUGH CATHEDRAL.[1] In the east bay of the north aisle of the nave is a beast's head on the intersection of the Norman vaulting-ribs (178). In the high vault of the western bay of the nave the angles between the ribs are ornamented with trefoil foliage, the centre of the boss not being carved but having a small hole (179); this is a way of ornamenting the keystone that I have not found elsewhere. There are two more thirteenth-century bosses at each end of the quire aisles, but only ordinary foliage. In the great west porch there are early thirteenth-century bosses, but they are badly weathered.

In the quire are a large number of late fifteenth-century wooden bosses; these are more or less rectangular plates which are probably bolted onto the wooden roof. Among the subjects are the Crucifixion, Resurrection, Temptation, Trinity, Annunciation, and Assumption. There are a large number of beasts and birds, among them the seven-headed beast of the Apocalypse; also two dragons with intertwined necks, as found so often in the West country; there are also heads and coats of arms.

Under the tower are many wooden bosses, some modern, but some I think may be from the fourteenth-century lantern, and were replaced when the present tower was rebuilt in 1884–6.

In the late fourteenth-century west porch are two remarkable bosses, a Trinity and an Assumption (180-81). In the sixteenth-century New Building are a number of coats of arms with borders of foliage.

PETERBOROUGH, ST JOHN THE BAPTIST.[2] In the south porch are two fifteenth-century bosses, an Annunciation and a Trinity; they are both good, but rather weathered.

PLUSCARDINE PRIORY. A number of bosses, some dating from the first half of the thirteenth century; most are foliage, with some good early trefoil.

[1] C. J. P. Cave, 'The Roof Bosses of Peterborough Cathedral', *Archaeologia*, vol. LXXXVIII, p. 271.
[2] C. J. P. Cave, 'The Roof Bosses in the Church of St John the Baptist, Peterborough', *Archaeologia*, vol. LXXXVIII, p. 277.

An Agnus Dei, a pelican feeding its young in the nest, and a rather grotesque face are probably fifteenth-century. In the Dunbar vestry is a late boss with the arms of Dunbar supported on the dexter by Queen Margaret with sceptre and book, and on the sinister by St Andrew.

PLYMOUTH, ST ANDREW. This church had many bosses of the ordinary Cornish and west Devon types; in a number of cases all the bosses on the same rib were of similar design.

PLYMPTON, ST MARY. Wagon roofs with more or less rectangular bosses, including the Virgin and Child, SS Peter and Paul, the arms of the Augustinian priory of Plympton and of the see of Exeter. In the porch are some stone bosses; one has a Crucifixion with a figure on either side represented as standing on brackets, the whole perhaps meant to represent the figures over the rood-screen; round are other bosses with angels holding shields; there are also two heads with mouth foliage.

POLING, SUSSEX. Wooden bosses said to have come from the FitzAlan Chapel at Arundel (*q.v.*).

PORTSMOUTH CATHEDRAL. Two bosses in the north aisle of the quire in the Chichester-Boxgrove style. The bosses in the high vault of the quire are I think nineteenth-century.

PORTSMOUTH, SS JOHN AND NICHOLAS (GARRISON CHAPEL). The first and third bosses are early conventional foliage in the Chichester-Boxgrove style; the middle boss is later, being naturalistic vine, but with no fruit.

POUGHILL, CORNWALL. Wagon roof with some very curious heads with pleated head-dress; also some good conventional foliage.

QUEEN CAMEL, SOMERSET.[1] Extremely good wooden bosses on the wagon roof of the chancel with numerous subjects from the bestiaries. There is a fine foliate head at the east end of the north aisle.

[1] For a full description see article by G. C. Druce, F.S.A., in the *Proceedings of the Somersetshire Archaeological and Natural History Society*, vol. LXXXIII, p. 88 (1937).

RIPON CATHEDRAL.[1] A series of fourteenth-century wooden bosses in the quire come probably from the old roof of the quire, not from the nave as sometimes maintained. They were repaired and gilded during Gilbert Scott's restoration in 1862–70. Photographs taken when the bosses had been taken down show that considerable repairs took place, but on the whole it was not badly done. The Crucifixion is modern. The old bosses are the Annunciation, a bishop standing, another seated, a king and a bishop seated side by side, Christ in Glory, a seated figure with a crown, now with wings but probably not so originally, a head of Christ, the Creation of Adam, God speaking to Eve after the Fall, and the Expulsion; also two heads. There are some later small bosses in the transepts, one being an Agnus Dei.

ROCHESTER CATHEDRAL. Under the tower are four large heads with mouth foliage; the roof of the crossing has been more than once remade, and it is extremely doubtful if these four bosses are medieval; one of them is a very close copy of a head in the north transept; the other three, if nineteenth-century, must have been copied from medieval models. There is a great number of foliate heads in the quire aisles and in the transepts. The bosses in the Early English style in the quire are modern, except perhaps the eastern one.

SALISBURY CATHEDRAL. Very beautiful thirteenth-century bosses in quire, transepts and nave; all are foliage except a few in the nave aisles which have dragons among the foliage (186-9). Under the tower are later bosses, all foliage, except one which is a foliate head.

In the chapter-house there are also foliage bosses, but there are figures on some of them.

In the cloisters, though most of the bosses are foliage only, there are quite a number of figures and heads, including a very youthful demi-figure of Christ.

There is a very large series of corbel heads in the triforium; some of these heads are exceptionally good.

SALLE, NORFOLK.[2] A fine series of wooden bosses fastened to the roof timbers up the centre of the chancel; the subjects from the west end are: the Annunciation, Adoration of the Shepherds, Circumcision, Adoration of the

[1] C. J. P. Cave, 'The Roof Bosses in Ripon Cathedral', *Archaeologia*, vol. LXXXVIII, p. 277.

[2] C. J. P. Cave, 'The Roof Bosses in the Chancel of Salle Church', *Norfolk and Norwich Archaeological Society*, vol. XXV, p. 368.

Magi, Triumphal Entry, Last Supper, Crucifixion, Resurrection, and Ascension. These bosses are of a very high artistic merit; unfortunately some of them are very badly worm-eaten (190-3). The nave has a number of wooden bosses, including archangels, angels with shields, and foliage bosses with small figures in the centre.

In the porch is a stone boss of Christ coming in judgement; the figure of Christ is surrounded by angels, and there are some Passion emblems; the whole is surrounded by conventional clouds.

SAMPFORD BRETT, SOMERSET. Wagon roof with wooden bosses in nave; there are several beasts, some rather in the Queen Camel style; antelope, stallion, goat, a griffin eating a bird, an eagle, dragons (one boss has two with intertwined necks). In the chancel are foliage and geometrical patterns; in the north transept are square bosses with foliage. The wall-plate in the nave has a series of cherubs' heads with some vine foliage above; they are very effective, but are probably modern.

SAMPFORD COURTENAY, DEVON. All wagon roofs except the south aisle of the nave which is flat. A very fine series of wooden bosses. In the chancel are two exceptionally fine bearded heads, one with mouth foliage; there is also a queen's head, a foliate woman's head, and three rabbits with only three ears between the three (182-5, 316-17). In the nave there are heads of a king and queen rather in the style of North Bovey, a bearded man with a high head-dress, a woman's head with mouth and eye foliage, a sow and farrow, and another example of the three rabbits. The Courtenay arms appear several times.

ST SAMPSON, CORNWALL. Wagon roofs with wooden bosses in chancel, nave and south aisle; some fine examples of Cornish foliage. The bosses in the eastern part are better than those at the west end, and are of a different kind of wood, or at any rate of a different colour; there are two Passion emblem bosses, one in the nave and one in the aisle, both with Cross, hammer and pincers, and Crown of Thorns surrounding them. Both purlines and rafters are richly ornamented.

SELBY ABBEY. In the nave are over sixty square wooden bosses; these had been bolted through the wooden roof, and when the fire occurred the wooden pins being burnt first caused the bosses to fall; many were not much damaged and were replaced when the new roof was put up. A great number of these bosses seem to be medieval; some can be seen in photographs to have been damaged, and some to have been repaired; only a few have the appearance of being modern. There is a variety of subjects: birds, beasts, fish, a centaur, a mermaid, rabbits, a man with a sword riding an ass, an elephant and castle, an ape, a wild boar under an oak tree, two bears fighting with staves and targets, a wild man, and foliage, some of it naturalistic, or with a naturalistic tendency (194-201). There is also an Agnus Dei.

There are stone bosses in the north aisle of the quire, several foliate heads, and a naked figure at the east end. In the sacristy is an angel holding a mitre.

SELWORTHY, SOMERSET. Very remarkable wooden bosses; those in the chancel and nave are rectangular or square plates with figures on them. The chancel bosses do not seem to me to be medieval. Those in the nave include a Trinity, the Father holding the Crucifix, with no Dove, a Virgin and Child, the Evangelists, three being represented holding an open book and a scroll, with their emblem below, St Matthew represented by an angel with an open book and a scroll; there are also St Peter, St Paul, St Christopher, and St Katherine. All the chancel and nave bosses have been recoloured, it is said about 1870. In the south aisle there is a very rich wagon roof with eighty bosses; all are foliage except those on the ninth cross beam from the east; these have shields with Passion emblems. In the north aisle there are also bosses, but mostly foliage.

SHEPTON MALLET, SOMERSET. A very remarkable wagon roof in the nave with 306 wooden bosses, and 18 half-bosses; nearly all are foliage, but there are a few heads, two of them foliate, of which one has stems not only from the mouth but from the eyeballs also.

The roof is divided into 350 panels, each ornamented with foliage, shields, or geometrical patterns; the whole effect is extremely rich. The wagon roof of the chancel is modern, and there are no bosses in the aisles.

SHERBORNE ABBEY. Very rich fan-vaulting with a great number of bosses. These include a foliate head with leaves and bunches of grapes, an archer shooting with a cross-bow at the rump of another man, a mermaid, a Passion emblem, a pelican, an owl mobbed by other birds, St Michael and the Dragon, and many others, including the rebus of Abbot Ramsam several times (202-9).

SHOREHAM (NEW), SUSSEX. Very early bosses with trefoil foliage. In the high vault of the quire two of the bosses have the ribs crossing the keystone with no foliage; in one bay there is a flat plaque with no carving on it. But the most curious bosses are in the aisles where there are angle heads with mouth foliage that goes down to the underside of the boss, so that from immediately below the head is invisible and the appearance is that of an ordinary foliage boss.

SHREWSBURY, SALOP. There is a number of bosses on the wooden roofs of chancel and nave; those in the chancel may be old ones touched up; many of those in the nave are modern, put up after the fall of the spire in 1894 when the roof of the nave was destroyed; but I have reason to suppose that most of the angels with musical instruments are originals, saved from the early roof, slightly restored and given new wings.

[SILKSTONE, YORKS.] Some very good wooden bosses; several heads, two of them with mouth foliage; four heads on one boss, chin to chin, all with protruding tongues; an angel bearing a shield with Passion emblems, the pillar, hammer and pincers.

SOMERTON, SOMERSET. A very rich, low, king-post roof with a great many wooden bosses, but nearly all foliage.

SOUTHWARK CATHEDRAL. There are five bosses in the quire, four of which I think are early thirteenth-century in spite of the fact that the roof was rebuilt about 1820; there is a tradition that some old material was used at that time. The boss at the west end of the quire seems a little later and it may have belonged to the original nave. The first four bosses consist of unusual foliage; there are some grotesque heads on one, and angle heads on at least two others.

In the south aisle of the quire are a number of fifteenth-century wooden bosses that came from the destroyed nave; amongst others are Judas being chewed by the Devil, a pelican, the arms of the City of London, and a rebus (293, 324, 325).

SOUTHWELL MINSTER. There is a considerable number of thirteenth-century bosses in the quire, almost all foliage, though two or three of them have dragons; they are extremely good. In the chapter-house there are foliage bosses which are not trefoil and which seem to be later than the naturalistic period.

SPREYTON, DEVON. In the chancel there are bosses with A, ω and ℥, which may be modern; also a head with mouth and eye foliage, and three rabbits with three ears between them (this occurs again in the nave).

There is a long inscription on the rafters in the chancel; it says that Henry Le Moyne, vicar, wrote it with his own hand; he was vicar from 1445 to 1458.

STAMFORD ST MARY, LINCS. In the north chantry is a wagon roof with 380 bosses; a large number, perhaps the majority, are foliage, but there are a large number of heads, etc. There are several grotesque heads in the nave.

STOODLEIGH, DEVON. Nave with wagon roof with bosses that have modern colouring, red and white. The bosses are peculiar and very crude, and are unlike any I have come across elsewhere. There are no less than four mermaids; a number of heads with beards growing under the chin; two examples of birds, perhaps swans, with their necks intertwined; also a mitre. In a number of cases the boss on the north side is repeated on the corresponding boss on the south. The chancel roof is modern with Passion emblems resembling those at St Neot, etc. (294).

STRATFORD-SUB-CASTLE, WILTS. Wagon roofs with many bosses; those in the chancel seem to be older than those in the nave. The nave has a number of wall-plate bosses with curious figures of uncertain date, but probably very late. Some of the figures carry shields; one has a remarkable coat of arms, a bear mounted on a ragged staff and plucking a rose (295).

STRATTON, CORNWALL. Wagon roofs with wooden bosses, one with the arms of Jerusalem, but the cross is in saltire. There are several heads with pleated head-dresses, several birds, some good foliage, and several large round bosses enclosing a cusped circle with a rose in the centre.

SUTTON, CAMBS. Some late but fairly good wooden bosses under the tower, including evangelistic symbols, several heads, and several angels, one carrying a crown, another a shield charged with three crowns. One boss has a crowned lion and a chained and collared antelope (?) both sejant, with a crown between them.

TAVISTOCK, DEVON. Wagon roofs with 210 bosses; on the wall-plate in the south aisle are forty-four angels, probably much restored. Almost all the bosses are foliage, but in the north aisle of the chancel there is a rather good head of a woman in a reticulated head-dress; also three rabbits with only three ears between them, and the arms of Lacy, Bishop of Exeter (1420–55). In the chancel are some good nineteenth-century bosses.

TAWTON (NORTH), DEVON. Wagon roofs with 197 bosses, all foliage; There is a marked tendency for all the bosses on the same rafter to be similar, as in a number of other West country churches.

TAWTON (SOUTH), DEVON. Wagon roofs in nave and chancel, and nearly flat roofs in the aisles. Some very good wooden bosses, including some remarkable foliate heads with foliage from the nose as well as from the mouth; among others is a boss with three rabbits with only three ears between them, a two-headed eagle, an owl, the heads of a man and a woman kissing, the head of a king, a spiral that may be meant for a maze, and a very typical sheila.

TEWKESBURY ABBEY.[1] A magnificent collection of bosses. In the nave is the Life of Christ, early fourteenth-century; beginning at the west end the subjects are the Nativity, Circumcision, the Magi on their journey, the Adoration of the Magi, the Finding in the Temple, the Triumphal Entry, the Last Supper, the Betrayal, the Scourging, the Crucifixion, the Resurrection, the Ascension, Pentecost, the Coronation, and Christ in Glory. North and south of the central line are angels, censing, playing musical instruments, and holding Passion emblems. On the elaborate roof of the quire are foliate heads, the Vernicle held by an angel, and many foliage bosses. There are a number of heads on the vaulting-ribs of the quire in unusual positions. Under the tower are numerous foliage bosses, also two shields of arms, and a lion and a dragon fighting.

In the ambulatory and apsidal chapels are foliate heads, a Coronation, the Martyrdom of King Edmund, St Michael and the Dragon, a Resurrection, a panther surrounded by many beasts. In the transepts are a number of heads, mostly grotesque, and some foliate, and two stars in the midst of conventional clouds (210-21, 308).

THORNTON ABBEY, LINCS. Some late fourteenth- or early fifteenth-century bosses under the gatehouse; most of them are large; there are foliate heads, and one very fine bearded head.

[1] C. J. P. Cave, 'The Roof Bosses in the Nave of Tewkesbury Abbey', *Archaeologia*, vol. LXXIX, p. 73.

THORVERTON, DEVON. Bosses in the porch; in the centre is a unique representation of the Trinity; the Father wrapped in a large cloak is holding the Son in front of him, as in the representations of the Trinity where the Son is shown on the Cross; but here there is no Cross; the Son is blessing and has a nimbus of radiating lines; below and upside down compared with the other figures is a winged figure. At the base of the boss, that is, above the head of the winged figure, is a vesica piscis within which an eyeball has been painted and which may not have been originally meant for an eye. On other bosses are the four doctors of the church and the evangelistic symbols; also a demi-figure of a man holding a small cross in front of him and gazing open-mouthed at the central boss.

TICKENCOTE, RUTLAND. A remarkable Norman boss on the sexpartite vaulting of the chancel; it is a circular plaque with three heads, one human and two beasts (1).

TYNEMOUTH PRIORY. There are a number of bosses in the Percy Chapel; they are all flat plaques, mostly with figures. They include a head of Christ; Christ with the vexillum and a kneeling figure, probably the 'Noli me tangere', a seated figure, Christ in Glory with two censing angels, St James seated, a standing figure; other bosses have evangelistic symbols, and apostles.[1]

UGBOROUGH, DEVON. The bosses in the chancel and its aisles are probably all modern. Those in the north aisle of the nave, on a flat panelled roof, are old; they have a striking likeness to those at Sampford Courtenay and South Tawton. They include foliate heads, a sow and farrow, a man and woman kissing, and St Eloy forging a horse shoe.

WALPOLE ST PETER, NORFOLK. Some very good animal bosses in the porch, including dogs gnawing bones, wild boars, a lion, a bear chained and muzzled, and others. There are also an Assumption and Last Judgement. Above the stalls in the chancel are numerous unusual miniature bosses, heads and foliage.

WARMINGTON, NORTHANTS. A very remarkable Early English wooden roof imitating stone vaulting (compare the cloisters at Lincoln). The bosses are

[1] See Gibson's *History of the Monastery of Tynemouth*.

well carved; they are mostly heads, many foliate, one having stems from the eyes, one from the nostrils. In the north aisle are some Cromwellian bosses; one bears the date 1650, and another initials (302, 303).

WARWICK, BEAUCHAMP CHAPEL.[1] Over the east window is God the Father, with the hierarchies of angels in the mouldings forming the frames of the window (compare St George's Chapel, Windsor). In the vaulting of the chapel are other bosses, including an Assumption. There are many very beautiful bosses, consisting below of flat plaques with geometrical designs, from which foliage grows up over the vaulting-ribs; some of the foliage is in the late naturalistic style.

WELLS CATHEDRAL. In the high vault of quire, nave and transepts all the bosses are foliage, except one in the south transept which bears two dragons. In the Lady Chapel is a Christ in Glory, with attendant angels; the colouring is modern and there may have been some modern restoration. There are some beasts on some of the bosses in the nave aisles. In the undercroft are some foliate heads, evangelistic symbols, and human figures with dragons near them; there is also an Agnus Dei. In the chapter-house there is some good naturalistic foliage, and some finely carved foliate heads.

There are many bosses in the cloisters, but all are weathered, some badly and it is difficult to interpret many of them. In the west walk there is a miller with a sack over his shoulder and a water-wheel close by, a man cutting down a tree, a bagpipe player, several heads, some grotesque, three men at stool (on one boss) and two sheilas of an unusual type. There are several bosses with cressets, the badge of Bishop Beckington (1443–65). In the south walk there are many angels, four together on one boss, some holding shields of arms, on one boss holding a scroll, and on another a rose. There are also single angels holding shields with Passion emblems.

WELLS, ST CUTHBERT. On the fine Somerset-style wooden roof are angels with shields, some of them with Passion emblems painted on them; these paintings are certainly modern and the whole of the figures may be. In St Cuthbert's Chapel are two lions with feet like those of birds, and a fine rose

---

[1] Philip B. Chatwin, F.S.A., 'The Decoration of the Beauchamp Chapel, Warwick', *Archaeologia*, vol. LXXVII, p. 313.

surmounted by a crown. Under the tower is the demi-figure of an archangel with hands in an attitude of prayer. In the porch are some good bosses including two beasts fighting, a sow and farrow, a foliate head, and a 'toothache' face.

WESTMINSTER ABBEY. These bosses are among the most important in the country. In the high vault of the quire and transepts the bosses are all foliage and nearly all trefoil, but in the transepts there are a few examples of the naturalistic style. The bosses in the quire aisles and in the adjoining chapels and in the east aisles of the transepts are mostly foliage of an early character, but there are a few figures among them, such as dragons in the foliage in the east aisle of the north transept, and angels in the angles of a boss in the north quire aisle; the large rose in the east aisle of the north transept, and the marguerite in the north aisle of the quire are obviously modern, and can be seen to be bolted on, probably to replace a broken boss; they are probably wooden. The bosses in the west aisle of the north transept and in the muniment room are extremely interesting, being very early examples of figure bosses. Some are badly weathered and are broken; the figures are David playing a harp, the Annunciation (226), an old man and a young man, possibly a prophet and an apostle, two bearded figures sitting side by side, both headless; another headless figure is almost certainly the Virgin with the Child, and yet another probably the souls of the just in Abraham's bosom; another figure is too much mutilated to see what it is meant for. In the muniment room itself are three magnificent bosses; they are different in style from the rest of the bosses in the transept and are of an extremely high artistic merit. One represents a centaur, or half-man, half-lion fighting with a winged amphisbaena (230), another a man and a merman fighting, the third a coiled dragon biting a man in the thigh.

In the high vault of the first four bays west of the tower the naturalistic style predominates, with examples of ivy, yellow water-lily, ranunculus, pennywort, vine, hawthorn, oak, maple, and rose. From the evidence of the bosses it looks as though a little time must have elapsed between the erection of this vaulting and that further to the east. The first five bays of the aisles west of the crossing belong to the same period as the first four bays of the high vault, they may even be slightly earlier. Some of the bosses here are interesting; a centaur half-hidden in foliage is shooting an arrow upwards and there are angle heads to this boss; a man's head, with an expression of agony on his face, is surrounded by lions, two of them are tearing at his hair, two clawing at his breast; a cock is half-hidden in foliage on another boss (227-8).

Further west, as would be expected, there is an abrupt change in style; on the high vault most of the bosses are conventional foliage, but there is one of two angels supporting a blank shield, and holding a crown over it; we also find the arms of Edward the Confessor, and the arms of the Abbey, both ancient and modern; the boss at the western end, a portcullis, must belong to the Tudor period. In the aisles the bosses are of the same character as those in the high vault; there are a few figures, and near the west end of the north aisle are two grotesque heads (229).

It remains to mention a very charming little fifteenth-century boss of the Assumption in the chapel of Our Lady of the Pew (232). Also the magnificent pendant bosses in Henry VII's Chapel (231) and their very attractive little counterparts in the aisles of the chapel (233-4). In the vestibule to the chapel the ceiling is divided into compartments in whose centres are small bosses, conventional foliage, badges, angels and animals.

The bosses in the destroyed vaulting over the crossing were nineteenth-century; this, the only part of the vaulting that was destroyed by enemy action, was the only vaulting in the Abbey that was not medieval.

The figures in the thirteenth-century choir of angels on the soffits of the lancet-windows in the north transept are not strictly roof bosses (222-5).[1]

WESTMINSTER, CHAPEL OF ST MARY. This crypt, all that remains of the Chapel of St Mary, has a large number of bosses; they have been much restored and repainted, but I am under the impression that they are fundamentally medieval work of about 1320. 'With the exception of the vaulting and possibly some of the supporting shafts the whole face work is modern.'[2] Down the centre of the roof are five large bosses representing St John in the cauldron of oil, St Laurence on the gridiron, St Margaret virgin and martyr, St Katherine of Alexandria, St Stephen. There are some angels with musical instruments, and a number of heads of men and beasts, some of them foliate.

WESTMINSTER, ST STEPHEN'S CLOISTERS. A number of very good Tudor bosses, including St Stephen, Christ in Glory, Virgin and Child, arms of

---

[1] C. J. P. Cave and L. E. Tanner, 'A Thirteenth-Century Choir of Angels in the North Transept of Westminster Abbey and the Adjacent Figures of Two Kings', *Archaeologia*, vol. LXXXIV, p. 63.

[2] *Royal Commission on Historical Monuments, London*, vol. II, p. 123.

Henry VII, Edward III, the Confessor, and Cardinal Wolsey; a number of angels bearing shields, some with Passion emblems, and many others. Eleven of the twenty-six bays were completely destroyed by enemy action, and two more were partially destroyed; but fourteen bosses from these bays have been recovered from the ruins, and with one exception these have hardly been damaged (235-8).

WIDECOMBE-IN-THE-MOOR, DEVON. Wagon roof with numerous wooden bosses in chancel and nave; among others are a demi-figure of Christ in Glory, St Katherine, an antelope, a good bearded head, several foliate heads, pelicans (twice), three rabbits with three ears between them, a lion rampant. These are all of West-country types, and some are rather like South Tawton examples.

WILSHAMSTEAD, BEDS. There are a number of wooden bosses in the nave, some with foliage, some with birds and beasts; a number of them have labels; amongst them are a stag, antelope, unicorn, eagle, lamb, and other beasts difficult to identify. The bosses are peculiar and quite different from the West-country wooden bosses.

WINCHESTER CATHEDRAL.[1] By far the finest bosses in the Cathedral are the wooden bosses in the quire put up quite early in the sixteenth century under Bishop Fox. They consist of Passion emblems at the east end, royal arms and badges in the centre, and the arms of Fox and of the four sees he held in succession at the west end. The collection of Passion emblems is the most important in the country. In the stone vaulting of the quire aisles are bosses of about the same date with Fox's arms, Tudor badges, Passion emblems, etc.

In the retroquire are a few thirteenth-century bosses, but mostly small and unimportant. On the high vault of the nave there are over 400 bosses, but nearly all of them are conventional foliage very finely carved but somehow lacking in inspiration; amongst them are a very few heads; in each bay there are four shields of arms, a cross, the see of Winchester, Wykeham, and the royal arms, some with France ancient, some with France modern. Over the windows

---

[1] C. J. P. Cave, 'The Bosses on the Vault of the Quire of Winchester Cathedral', *Archaeologia*, vol. LXXVI, p. 161; 'The Roof Bosses in the Nave Aisles, Winchester Cathedral', *Proceedings of the Hampshire Field Club and Archaeological Society*, vol. XII, p. 48; 'The Roof Bosses of Winchester Cathedral', *The Friends of Winchester Cathedral*, 1935.

are figures of men, semi-human creatures, and beasts; some have indications of deformity, and a few are definitely phallic.

The bosses in the nave aisles are much more interesting than those in the high vault. There are a large number of heads, some foliate, demi-figures, angels with shields of arms, others with musical instruments, a sow and farrow where the sow itself is being carried off by a lion, and perhaps strangest of all a dragon in the courtyard of a castle.

In the Lady Chapel are two large, late fifteenth-century bosses, one of Christ in Glory supported by archangels, the other of the Assumption, Our Lady being supported by angels. The other bosses in the Lady Chapel are foliage or coats of arms. In the various chantries are a number of bosses; in Wykeham's there are heads of men and beasts; in Beaufort's there is an angel holding a shield with the Cardinal's arms, but all very much restored; the same applies to Waynflete's chantry; Langton's has coats of arms and the bishop's rebus; Fox's has four coats of arms like some of the wooden bosses in the quire.

Very remarkable are the seventeenth-century bosses on the Laudian Gothic wooden vaulting under the tower, which is dated 1635; the bosses consist of coats of arms of bishops and peers, including Laud himself, of badges of England, Scotland, Ireland, and France, and the unique portrait boss of Charles I and his queen.

Though not roof bosses, it may be well to mention here the series of carved figures above the arches in the nave. Among all sorts of figures are numerous heads, all extremely well carved; one of these heads is Wykeham's; it is identified by having an angel on either side, one bearing a shield with the arms of the see, the other those of Wykeham; moreover, the head bears a strong resemblance to other figures of Wykeham. I feel convinced that a number of other heads, perhaps all of them, are meant for portraits, though exactly whom they are meant for there is no means of knowing (239-71).

WINCHESTER, COLLEGE CHAPEL. A number of heads, some of them foliate; the most striking boss is an oval plate bearing the arms of Wykeham, surmounted by a mitre, and surrounded by the garter; it bears a date 1822. The rest of the bosses seem to be medieval, though a good deal restored. In Thorburn's chantry the vaulting must have been rebuilt when the tower was rebuilt, but some of the old bosses were evidently used; some of these have initials; there are also the arms of Wykeham and Waynflete; also a fox carrying off a goose and an ape patting a man's head.

WINCHESTER COLLEGE, FROMOND'S CHANTRY.[1] A more interesting set of bosses than those in the chapel; besides a number of coats of arms, there are a head of Beaufort and various grotesques.

WINCHESTER, ST CROSS. There are two bosses in the quire, one with stiff foliage, the other with six grotesque heads; these bosses strike me as having perhaps been put up after the erection of the vaulting, after the manner of so many French bosses. In the nave three bosses with the arms of Beaufort, a shield with Passion emblems, and the arms of Wykeham. The *V. C. H. Hampshire*[2] states 'the arms of Beaufort indicate that the vault was not completed till the fifteenth century', but the photographs of the three bosses give indications that these bosses, like those in the quire, were put up after the vault had been built. In the south aisle there are three conventional foliage bosses, and in the north aisle a foliate head; all these appear to be fifteenth-century.

WINDSOR, ST GEORGE'S CHAPEL. In the quire is an extremely good collection of early sixteenth-century bosses; on the central line are large bosses with coats of arms, or Tudor badges, both with supporters, alternating with large pendant bosses; an outer line, both north and south, consists of coats of arms or badges all with surrounding garters; beyond these lines, going outwards to the windows, we get in each bay, and both to north and south, a portcullis, a fleur-de-lis, a white greyhound, and a red dragon; on bosses on either side of this line we get the letters H and K bound together by a cord.

At the east end over the window is a Trinity of very unusual design (see Chapter II, p. 24). In the mouldings of the window are the heavenly hierarchies as in the Beauchamp chapel at Warwick. Immediately to the west of the Trinity boss is a pendant with a pelican feeding its young on the lower face, and a mitre on its west side, obviously an allusion to Fox, bishop of Winchester and prelate of the Order of the Garter. In the quire aisles are angels holding shields; they look as though they had been considerably restored. At the east end of the south quire aisle is a representation of a king, Edward IV and a bishop, Beauchamp, bishop of Salisbury, kneeling before the Cross Naid, a famous relic.

In the centre of the crossing are the royal arms supported by a crowned lion and a griffin with the date 1528; other arms with the garter surround it.

[1] Herbert Chitty, F.S.A., 'Fromond's Chantry at Winchester College', *Archaeologia*, vol. LXXV, p. 139. The bosses are described and illustrated. [2] Vol. v, p. 63.

In the nave we find the Cross Naid again; there are also numerous animals, including white greyhounds and yales; several initials, among them the letter H partly formed out of a dragon, and the letter K crowned. There is a shield with Passion emblems, the arms of Sir Reginald Braye, and his device, the hemp bray, a number of times (272-83).

In the western transepts there is a boss with the initials of George IV surrounded by the garter.

WOOTTON COURTENAY, SOMERSET. Wagon roof; north aisle has good wooden bosses, many of birds and beasts of the Somerset type, also St George slaying the Dragon, a pelican in its nest with its young, and a head of Christ.

WORCESTER CATHEDRAL.[1] In the quire, Lady Chapel, and eastern transepts, which were dedicated in 1218, are seven figure bosses; these must be the earliest figure bosses in the country and should therefore be of great importance, but there were such drastic restorations at Worcester in the nineteenth century that suspicion rests on much of the sculpture in the Cathedral. Of these eastern bosses the Virgin and Child at the east end of the Lady Chapel is the least suspect, though it must have been restored; the next three bosses, archbishop, bishop, and king, and the boss of Christ in the quire may have a substratum of old work about them, but the figures in the eastern transepts representing the Old and the New Testaments are completely Victorian. Happily when we leave the quire, though signs of restoration are numerous, we are on safer ground. In the south main transept are two archbishops, one with censing angels; in the opposite transept is a 'Noli me tangere'. Under the tower are a number of heads. In the nave on the central line is a bishop with censing angels. On the bosses over the windows are a number of heads, some extremely fine; also some animals and a human figure which is definitely phallic.

In the north aisle of the nave are an Annunciation, Nativity, and Coronation; in the south aisle some good women's heads in pairs. Perhaps the most interesting bosses in Worcester are those in the cloisters; some are very much weathered; their date is the latter part of the fourteenth century. In the south

[1] Canon J. M. Wilson, 'Note on Some of the Bosses in the Cloisters of Worcester Cathedral and in Particular on the Jesse Tree in the South Cloister', *Reports and Papers read at the Meetings of the Architectural Societies*, vol. XXX, part 2, p. 578.

C. J. P. Cave, 'The Roof Bosses in Worcester Cathedral', *Transactions of the Worcestershire Archaeological Society* (1934), vol. XI, New Series, p. 75.

walk two series lead up to the Coronation of the Virgin in the centre; at the west end is Jesse, a recumbent figure with a tree springing from him; on the other bosses between Jesse and the Coronation is a succession of kings representing the line of Jesse. At the east end is another prone figure with a stem growing out of him, but he wears a mitre; between this boss and the centre we have a series of kings or others bearing scrolls; Wilson suggests[1] that this may represent a sort of spiritual genealogy. In the north walk there are archangels and angels, and some heads. The other walks contain a great number of bosses of a variety of subjects (284-91).

WORCESTER, St ANDREW.[2] Under the spire is a lierne vault with a central well-hole. The principal bosses depict the Annunciation, Adoration of the Magi, Triumphal Entry, Coronation; on other bosses are the Twelve Apostles. There is also a boss with a man and woman kneeling before a pope; they may have been the donors of the roof; there is also St George slaying the Dragon and some heads of which several are foliate. There are a few good foliage bosses in the chancel.

WORSTED, NORFOLK. A few wooden bosses, including an extremely well-carved figure over the font, holding a book with marks on it to represent writing; the figure may be meant for an angel, though now it has no wings. In the aisles are a king, a bird-of-prey eating another bird, a foliate monster, and some heads. In the south porch is a stone boss of the Coronation, rather worn.

WYMONDHAM, NORFOLK. In the nave large wooden bosses of flat, spreading, conventional foliage, some of which have faces or heads in the centre. In the porch are some stone bosses, all very much worn; in the centre is the Coronation; round it the Annunciation, Nativity, Resurrection, and perhaps the Ascension. There are also some angels, one playing a citole.

YEOVIL, SOMERSET. Some very good wooden heads; also a curious boss, almost a pendant, with a head on each face, all of them having mouth foliage; there is one shield with the arms of England quartering France modern painted on it; the painting looks modern.

[1] Loc. cit. p. 84.
[2] Rev. W. R. Buchanan-Dunlop, 'St Andrew's Church, Worcester', *Transactions of the Worcestershire Archaeological Society*, vol. XIV (New Series), p. 18.

YORK MINSTER. The wooden roofs of both quire and nave were destroyed by fire, the former in 1829, the latter in 1840. The loss of both is much to be deplored, but especially that of the nave, for wooden bosses of the Decorated period are not by any means common. Happily, Halfpenny in his *Gothic Ornaments in York Minster*, and Browne in his *History of the Metropolitan Church of St Peter, York*, have given many illustrations of the bosses in both parts of the Minster, and the modern bosses have largely been copied from their illustrations.

In the aisles of both quire and nave there are a number of bosses, but none that call for special mention. In the east aisle of the south transept there are two early bosses, one of St Michael slaying the Dragon, the other the Agnus Dei. In the high vault of the transept where three vaulting-ribs abut onto the wall-plate there are two bosses shaped like the segment of a circle, one with merman and mermaid, the other with winged beasts with human heads; there were a number of similarly shaped bosses in the nave, with grotesque creatures. In the centre of the tower vaulting is a boss with two figures, one a king holding a church, the other an old man holding a book.

In the chapter-house there is an Agnus Dei and another in the vestibule. The other chapter-house bosses are foliage, mostly naturalistic, one of them has small heads and another beasts amidst the foliage.

Under the quire screen is a small but very good Assumption, with modern painting. On the front of the screen are thirty very small bosses beautifully carved; the subjects include the Ascension, Baptism in the Jordan, Annunciation, Coronation, St Michael (twice), the Evangelistic symbols, and many angels. In the centre of the screen are two angels, one playing, and one blowing a portative organ.

YORK, GUILDHALL. This was destroyed during an air raid in 1942. There were a number of fifteenth-century wooden bosses; they were mostly heads, some foliate; among others were an angel bearing a shield with a merchant's mark, a griffin, a bagpipe player; the bust of a man holding up a flask had a modern appearance.

PHOTOGRAPHIC METHODS

ROOF BOSSES cannot be studied without optical aid. Modern prismatic field-glasses are not the best means to use, unless they are night-glasses, for the roofs are often so dark that details cannot be made out except in exceptionally light buildings like the quire at Winchester. I have found that small opera-glasses with a large aperture are far better than more powerful prismatic field-glasses.

But it is only by photography that roof bosses can really be studied; a mass of notes is far less satisfactory than a set of photographs; here we have a permanent record which can be studied at leisure. Points often come out in photographs that would certainly have been missed by a visual examination. But for photography a good telephoto lens is a necessity. These are of two kinds: one is a combination of a negative and a positive lens with a variable separation between the two lenses which allows a variable magnification to be obtained. These lenses have the advantage that one can photograph objects of various sizes and at various distances and yet make the object fit the size of the plate by altering the magnification. One disadvantage is that these lenses work at a small aperture and to ensure sharpness it is advisable to stop down; thus the exposures are long. Another disadvantage is that when a subject is not too well lighted, as is often the case, the image cannot be seen on the ground-glass screen; in this case a sighting telescope may be attached to the camera to centre the object on the plate. An indirect method of focusing is necessary, too. I have found that a convenient way is to focus on an electric torch placed as far away from the camera as the roof is above it. In most cathedrals the height of the vaulting can be given by a verger, but it is as well to measure it oneself, and for this purpose a small box sextant is useful. The simplest way to make the measurement is to go to such a distance from the camera that the elevation of the point of the roof above the camera is 45°; one is then at the same distance from the camera as the roof is above it. The same electric torch can be used for centering the sighting telescope which should have a centering adjustment. But when the camera is in a horizontal position the rather heavy telephoto lens may cause a certain amount of sag on the front of the camera which disappears when the camera is again brought to a vertical position, and the centering telescope is now out of adjustment. The remedy for this is to clamp the lens very firmly to the camera; this can be done very satisfactorily with an Atkin Swan tilting-table, which is useful in other ways, too. All these drawbacks sound rather formidable, but the advantages are that the lens is quite portable and does not require a very special camera as long as the latter has sufficient extension.

The telephoto lens with a fixed separation between the positive and negative lenses has the advantage of working at a much larger aperture so that the image is visible on the ground-glass screen and focusing can be done directly. Lenses working at $f/8$ may be obtained with an equivalent focal length of 36–40 in. and nothing much less than this is advisable for bosses on vaulting 60 ft. or more above the floor. These lenses are very bulky and heavy, but they give excellent results. They have two principal disadvantages: they practically require a special camera for work on bosses, and they have to be supplemented by, say, a 20 in. lens, as bosses low down or exceptionally large may more than cover the plate when taken with the longer focus lens.

The camera need have no complications of shutters, for exposures are best made with a cap; but the camera should have a mirror and a second ground-glass screen, as in a reflex camera; without this it is extremely difficult to focus when the camera is pointed vertically upwards. But the mirror need have no spring arrangement, a simple hand-lever is all that is necessary to work it.

The stand for both kinds of lens should be one that enables the camera to be pointed easily vertically upwards. For the camera carrying the 40 in. lens I use a Debrie tripod which, with a slight addition to the camera, allows a photograph to be taken in any direction from the horizontal to the vertical.

One other addition to the apparatus is extremely useful: a large triangle has holes at its angles to receive the feet of the tripod and the whole triangle is mounted on small rubber-tyred wheels; by this means the whole camera can be as wheeled about into any position. This arrangement saves a great deal of time, the camera can be moved from one position to another with the greatest ease.

Another piece of apparatus which is almost a necessity if much work is to be done is a spotlight. Many roofs receive so little light from the outside that without artificial light exposures have to be very long. It would have been quite impossible to photograph the choir of angels in the north transept of West-minster Abbey without a spotlight. The lamp used for most of the photographs I have taken is the Aldis Daylight Signalling Lamp, worked off a twelve-volt battery. Lamp and battery are mounted on a wheeled base so that, like the camera, they can be easily wheeled into any position. The beam of light is not quite parallel, but has a certain spread. The result of this is that the spot of light is more intense on low vaulting than on high. The relative exposures have to be worked out for the special lamp used.

Fast plates are advisable if much work is to be done, and when working with a spotlight a plate should be chosen which is sensitive to artificial light. In practice I have found Ilford Soft Gradation Panchromatic Plates all that could be desired. As to actual exposures, I have found that with these plates and a lens aperture of $f/11$ about one minute is required for a boss 70 ft. above the floor when there is little daylight on the roof.

The photographic apparatus described above has been very nearly superseded by the coming of the miniature camera. With a Leica camera and a 400 mm. lens one can get negatives which will enlarge up to 12 × 10 in. with hardly any sign of grain or loss of sharpness. Those who have worked with both will appreciate the lightness of the newer equipment compared with the old. Modern long-focus lenses for miniature cameras can be used at a large aperture; little advantage is gained by stopping down when photographing such things as roof bosses where no great depth of focus is necessary. Exposures can therefore be cut down considerably, and can be still further reduced as the films that can be used for miniature cameras are very fast.

As an example of speed in working I may mention that with a Leica camera, a 400 mm. lens and a spotlight I took 115 photographs in St Mary, Bury St Edmunds, in one morning and one hour of the afternoon. This may be compared with the two years that it took me to photograph the 97 bosses in the quire in Winchester Cathedral with a telephoto lens of variable separation between positive and negative lenses, and without a spotlight.

INDEX

Figures in heavy type refer to plates

THE ROYAL TECHNICAL COLLEGE
LIBRARY
GLASGOW

coll. H.

THE ROYAL TECHNICAL COLLEGE
LIBRARY
GLASGOW